Scats
and
Tracks
of the
Rocky Mountains

A Field Guide to the Signs of Seventy Wildlife Species

SECOND EDITION

James C. Halfpenny, Ph.D.
Illustrated by Todd Telander

FALCON®

Guilford, Connecticut
An imprint of The Globe Pequot Press

_A_FALCONGUIDE®

Copyright © 2001 by The Globe Pequot Press
Previous edition of this book was published by Falcon Publishing, Inc.
in 1998.

Cover photo by Michael S. Sample.

Library of Congress Cataloging-in-Publication Data is available.

ISBN 0-7627-1241-4

♻ Text pages printed on recycled paper

Manufactured in the United States of America
Second Edition/Fifth Printing

*To Diann, my alpha partner,
ursophile, and tracking friend, for
all her loving support and help.*

Acknowledgments

First and foremost, I wish to thank all my students for their years of questions and help, but most of all for the time we've shared tracking and studying in the field. I also wish to thank Larry Marlow, Terry McEneany for his help with bird tracks, and Susan Morse (Keeping Track, Jericho, Vermont) for her help with lynx and their footprints.

Contents

Introduction

In the late 1970s, the era of "watchable wildlife" arrived in the United States. Baby boomers wanted to turn to and experience the outdoors. Television brought wildlife closer than ever. Bird watching thrived. Now more than ever before, millions of people want to watch wildlife. Wild animals are not always easy to find and observe, though. Finding their tracks and signs is an exciting alternative to actually seeing the animals. "Trackable wildlife" adds another dimension to the outdoor experience. Todd and I wish to share that dimension, the joy of reading stories written in the soil and snow.

Upwards of ten books on tracking were written in the United States during each decade of the twentieth century. Most are general, covering the United States or all of North America. In *Scats and Tracks of the Rocky Mountains*, I focus on one biogeographic region, with details about the region's most common or characteristic species of mammals, birds, reptiles, and amphibians. (I have included a few rare species because of their particular interest or significance in a region. For example, what a coup it would be to document a Canada lynx in your favorite hiking area.) I've intentionally limited the number of species covered in order to keep the information manageable. This guide is small, allowing you to carry it in a pack or pocket and use it frequently.

As your knowledge and interest in tracking grow, you may want to find additional information. Key references are listed in Selected Reading. For a more detailed investigation of tracking, I recommend my book *A Field Guide to Mammal Tracking in North America* (1986, Johnson Publishing, Boulder, CO) and titles by Olaus Murie, L. R. Forrest, and Paul Rezendes.

One organization will, in computer parlance, provide interactive access to expand your tracking background. A

Naturalist's World (ANW) is an ecologically oriented company dedicated to providing educational programs and materials reflecting the natural history of North America. Diann Thompson and I run the daily business, teach classes, and lead programs. Our on-site classes provide hands-on experience and in-depth information about animals, their tracks, and the ecology of their environments. In addition to tracking classes, our field programs cover bears, wolves, winter ecology, the northern lights, and alpine ecology. ANW also provides books, videos, slides shows, and computer programs for self-study and as teaching and field aids. You can check out ANW on the internet at www.tracknature.com. Class schedules, product information, and information about ANW can be obtained by writing us at P.O. Box 989, Gardiner, Montana 59030, calling (406) 848-9458, or visiting us on the worldwide web at www.tracknature.com.

Keep on tracking!

—James C. Halfpenny

About tracking

Tracking is for everyone, beginner and expert, young and old. The fun of nature's challenge is solving the mystery written in the trail. Prepare yourself by learning the background and basics of tracking before exercising your skills in the field.

Field notes and preserving tracks

To the natural history detective, the track and trail are things of great beauty and significance. They tell part of the story of an animal's life. Tracks and trails deserve to be preserved, both to increase your knowledge and to serve as a record you can share with others. Preservation is commonly made in the form of written notes, casts, or photographs.

Perhaps the most important item in the naturalist's tool kit is the field notebook. Field notes can jog the memory and facilitate better retention of knowledge. The notes can be analyzed later and be preserved as records of chance encounters. Writing good field notes is both an art form and a science. Field notes are a source of pride when shown to others and may gain recognition for recording rare and unusual events. And need I mention how quickly memories, especially for details, fade when not preserved?

While great and complex systems have been designed for complete and accurate records, there are really but three requirements for the tracker: ruler, paper, and pen. With these, every trail becomes a record for later analysis and sharing. I cannot emphasize enough the importance of enhancing your tracking experience by keeping notes to which you can later refer!

A simple 3-by-5-inch notebook and a 6-inch ruler are adequate to get started. Use a pencil or a pen that won't run if your notes get wet. To facilitate taking notes, A Naturalist's World produces a waterproof notebook that contains information about footprint groups, gaits, and how to track; data sheets for recording information; and English and metric rulers imprinted on the back cover. See the Introduction for contact information for A Naturalist's World.

Tracks also may be preserved by photographing and making casts. Good photographs can be made by any modern camera that can take a good close-up. When taking pictures, try to fill the viewfinder with the footprint. Get as close as possible. Always include a ruler or some other object in the photo to provide a sense of scale. Avoid using hats, gloves, hands, or objects without a straight edge; round edges do not lend themselves to making accurate measurements from a photo. To avoid distortion, take the photograph from directly above the track, shooting straight down. Also, step back and take photographs of the trail to show the footprints that were photographed close up. Fast films (ASA of 200 or higher) are generally best, because tracks are often found in dark places, especially ground surfaces. Photographing the footprint with a GPS showing location adds authenticity.

Plaster casts are the old standby for preserving tracks. I suggest a casting kit that includes a 1-gallon (4-liter) plastic jar with a screw lid for carrying dry plaster, a narrow spatula, a plastic mixing cup such as those sold for medium-sized drinks, paper for wrapping and transporting the finished cast, and a plastic sack for cleanup. A bottle of water may be needed if water is not available on site. Two pounds of plaster will make at least four coyote-sized track casts.

Purchase plaster from a lumberyard or hardware store, as prices will be more reasonable than at a drugstore or hobby shop. Almost any plaster will work, including plaster of paris, hydrocal, ultracal, or hydrostone. Avoid getting plaster for wallboard or patching compound, however.

These plasters are formulated to be slightly flexible on walls and do not get hard enough for casts.

Two factors are critical to preventing casts from breaking: thickness and density. In the field, thickness is assured by building a wall around the track to contain the plaster. Natural objects such as twigs, stones, and dirt may be used to make a retaining wall 0.25–0.5 in (0.6–1.3 cm) above the track. Alternatively, walls in the form of plastic strips cut from milk cartons or other plastic containers may be taken to the field. Proper density is assured by mixing two parts of plaster to one part of water by volume (read instructions on plaster container) to create a mixture similar in consistency to thick pancake batter or a milkshake.

Place your spatula close to the track and pour the mixture onto the spatula to break the fall of the plaster into the footprint. Working quickly, so the plaster does not set and become too thick, gently pour the plaster first into the fine detailed areas of the footprint and then the rest of the print. Finally, pour the plaster to an appropriate depth (inside the retaining wall) to keep the cast from breaking. Vibrating the spatula up and down across the top of the plaster will cause it to settle evenly and create a smooth back for the cast.

Allow the plaster to dry for 30 minutes, or as long as is recommended on the plaster package. Gently pick the plaster up by digging your fingers under opposite sides of the cast, and turn the cast over onto one hand. Now wash off the dirt by rubbing the cast with your fingertips under the flowing water of a stream or a hose. Do not wash the cast in a sink as it may clog the drain. Let the cast continue to cure for several days in a warm, dry environment. If you need to transport it, wrap the cast in paper. Never wrap the cast in plastic as trapped moisture may cause it to crumble.

While special techniques are needed for dust and snow, this procedure will allow casting in many situations. Remember, carry a plastic garbage bag and *always* clean up your mess. No sign of your plaster should remain to reduce the experience of others who happen by later.

Scats and bird pellets

Scats and bird pellets (also called cough pellets or castings) are often helpful for identifying an animal or completing the story written in the trail. Scats and pellets help identify not only what the animal was eating but who the animal was. However, it should be noted that scats and pellets won't help you identify an animal with as much certainty as tracks will. Many animals make similar scats and pellets that are difficult to tell apart.

The scats of many carnivores are very similar, especially when the diet is mostly meat. Size alone does not provide a definitive answer because of the wide range of diameters produced within a species and even by a single member of a species. For example, fox produce scats ranging in size from 0.3–0.8 in (0.8–2 cm), coyotes produce scats from 0.5–1.3 in (1.3–3.3 cm), and wolves produce scats from 0.5–1.5 in (1.3–3.8 cm), and we all know how our own scat varies in size and shape. When judging size, consider both the total quantity of scat and the size of individual pieces. Moist food produces slimmer scats, while fibrous diets produce wider scats.

Given these cautions, scat shapes can be used to identify general groups of animals (see page xii). Spherical shapes flattened top to bottom are deposited by members of the rabbit order. Elongate spheres are deposited by rodents and shrews, and at larger sizes by deer and their relatives. Long, thick cords are deposited by dogs, bears, and raccoons. Dog scats typically have tapered ends, while those from bears and raccoons are blunt. Cats also produce thick cords with blunt ends, but they tend to be constricted or even broken into short segments. Cords that loop back on themselves are produced by members of the weasel family. Birds, in general, produce long, thin cords or shapeless, semiliquid excretions. Reptiles and amphibians may produce small elongate spheres or long, thin cords. White, nitrogenous urine deposits, found only on the scats of birds, reptiles, and amphibians, separate them from mammal scats.

Scats may be confused with cough pellets. Many bird groups, including owls, raptors, crows, ravens, jays, magpies, gulls, herons, storks, flycatchers, and kingfishers, produce cough pellets in addition to scats. Birds pass digestive juices through what they have eaten to remove the nutrients. Hair, bones, beaks, claws, and other non-digestible parts accumulate in the gizzard (anterior portion of stomach), are compressed, and are coughed up as pellets. Food remnants in the pellet are easy to identify and tell much about the bird's feeding habits and even the habitats it frequents.

cough pellet

Pellets are grayish in color and are spherical or long and tapered at both ends. When fresh, they are covered by mucus and appear dark black. Pellets are found mainly at roosting sites and nests, and occasionally at feeding areas. They are deposited singly, but many may accumulate beneath a tree where a bird is roosting, nesting, or perching. Nitrogenous scat deposits on the ground or twigs may help verify an object as a pellet.

The diameter of the throat determines the maximum diameter of the pellet. In general, large birds produce larger pellets. Shape and diameter allow one to distinguish to some degree between species.

Birds generally produce two pellets per day and regurgitate just before taking flight. The time of day when feeding occurred may affect the sample of food items. For example, owls tend to feed on mammals that come out only at night, while hawks feed on animals that are out during the daylight hours.

Shapes of scats

Spheres
Rabbits and their relatives

rabbit

Spheres, elongate
Rodents, shrews, deer, and their relatives

woodrat

shrew

elk

Cords, long and thick
Coyotes, bears, raccoons, and their relatives

coyote

bear

raccoon

Cords, thick and often constricted
Mountain lions and their relatives

mountain lion

Cords, often folded
Weasels and their relatives

mink

Cords, long and thin, often with nitrogenous deposits
Birds and reptiles

Canada goose

lizard

Anatomy and footprint nomenclature

The feet of mammals, birds, reptiles, and amphibians are anatomically complex, and that complexity shows in their footprints. Knowing something of the anatomy of their feet will aid in footprint identification and interpreting trails.

The toes of all animals are numbered from the inside of the foot out (the inside of the foot being the side closest to the animal). Therefore, in humans and other mammals, the thumb or big toe (if present) is number 1 and the little finger or little toe is number 5. In birds, toe 1 (if present) points backward.

Over evolutionary time, toes of animals have become reduced in size or have disappeared altogether. In cats and dogs, toe 1 is absent or reduced to a small toe called a *dewclaw*. In deer, elk, sheep, and similar mammals, toe 1 is absent and toes 2 and 5 are reduced and form dewclaws. Toes 3 and 4, the *clouts,* form the cloven *hoof.* In pronghorn antelope, toes 1, 2, and 5 are absent. In birds, toe 5 is absent and toe 1 is often reduced and occasionally absent. In the amphibians covered here, toe 1 has been lost from the front foot.

Track measurements

To more accurately determine the animal's foot size from its tracks, mountain lion researchers Fjelline and Mansfield (1989) developed the "minimum outline" method of measuring tracks.

Place your hand on a hard surface, a table for instance. Note the contact area of your hand with that surface. If your hand went no deeper into that surface, your handprint would have only one size—the *minimum outline.* If your hand were to sink deeper into the surface—as it would if the surface were, say, mud—it would create a series of variable outlines, each larger than the one before, as the mud flowed around the curved surface of your hand. All footprints have a minimum outline, but only prints that sink into a surface have variable outlines.

Note that while the variable outline of a footprint may only be several millimeters wider than the minimum outline, those few millimeters have a large visual effect. The human eye sees area, and area increases with the square of a linear measurement. In short, a few millimeters of width adds a lot of area to a footprint.

The minimum outline size does not change for different surfaces and therefore provides a standard for comparison between surfaces. And though one animal may leave many sizes of footprints depending on surface, slope, and speed, there is only one minimum outline for every footprint an animal might leave. The minimum outline measurement is the only constant and consistent size in tracking.

To measure the minimum outline, study the bottom of a print. The *break point* where the rounded pad turns upward is the edge of the minimum outline. Use this edge to measure tracks.

Assigning the break point is a subjective judgment, and no two people will always mark it at exactly the same point. However, testing has shown that an individual tracker using the minimum outline method can reduce personal variation in measurement and that groups of trackers using this method will also become more consistent in their measurement of tracks. Remember, the computer rule GIGO: gar-

cross section of footprint in ground

bage in, garbage out. You cannot get quality measurements from a bad track. Quality measurements are the tracker's goal, and using minimum outline methods greatly reduces over-exaggeration and variance in measurement.

All measurements in this guide are minimum outline measurements.

Averages

The measurements in *Scats and Tracks of the Rocky Mountains* are mostly averages gathered from years of tracking. Averages include only animals judged to be adult. However, it is important to remember the great size variation among animals. Every animal was small once in its life, and some never get big. Males are often substantially larger than females. Regional variations in mammal sizes also occur. For example, coyotes are smaller in the southwestern United States and larger in the northeastern part of the country. Their tracks vary accordingly. Therefore, a track in the field may be considerably larger or smaller than the measurements provided. Use track measurements only as a rough guideline, not as an absolute rule.

Gaits and trails

Coordinated muscle movements result in the various gaits used by animals. In the simplest form, when moving on two legs (bipedal movement) an organism can *walk, run,* and *hop.* When moving on four legs (quadrupedal movement) an organism can *walk, trot, lope, gallop, bound,* and *pronk* (also called *stot*). Though other gaits exist, I will confine our discussion to these basic gaits. Each gait leaves a characteristic pattern that may be modified by changes in speed and body angle. The combination of footprints is called the *trail.* The bipedal walk and run and the quadrupedal walk and trot result in gaits that are *symmetrical.* The right side of the trail is a mirror image of the left side. The trail patterns for these gaits are the same, alternating right-left pattern, and they differ only by the stride being longer in the run and trot than it is in the walk. In the run and trot, the straddle, the distance from the right edge of the rightmost pad (see page xix) to the left edge of the leftmost pad, also tends to be narrower than it is in the walk.

Quadrupedal movement also results in gaits that are *asymmetrical* (the right half of the trail is not always a mirror image of the left), including lope, gallop, bound, hop, and pronk. These gaits produce patterns that include all four footprints (two fronts, two hinds, two rights, and two lefts) in a group separated from the next group by a space where no footprints appear.

walk   **trot**

In *gallops,* the feet, front and rear, that move first (or *lead*) will determine whether the gallop will form a Z-shaped or C-shaped pattern. When the front and hind feet on the same side lead, the pattern takes on a Z shape. A right front lead with a left hind lead or vice versa results in a C-shaped pattern. Thus, there are four possible gallop patterns.

C-shaped gallop   **Z-shaped gallop**

Bounds (also known as hops and jumps) are characterized by the synchronization of the hind feet; both strike the ground at the same time, side by side. The front feet strike the ground at a different time than the hind feet. In a full bound, the front feet are synchronized and strike the ground

full bound   **half bound**

side by side at the same time. In a half bound, only the hind feet are synchronized and the front feet hit the ground staggered. Animals that mostly use full bounds, also called hops, live in trees (tree squirrels and songbirds), whereas those that mostly use half bounds live on the ground (ground squirrels and rabbits).

In a *pronk* (also called a *stot*), all four feet strike the ground at the same time, with the front feet side by side and forward of the hind feet, which are also side by side. This gait is often used by deer to gain height and increase time in the air to look around.

To increase peripheral vision, non-primate mammals have eyes placed toward the side of their heads, not flat on their face like humans. By turning sideways, a prey species can see what is pursuing it and where it needs to go to escape. The predator, by turning sideways, can see what it is chasing and where the rest of the predator pack is.

Consequently, quadrupedal mammals have evolved to use all gaits while their body is turned to the side. These *side gaits* result when the animal's heavy head deviates from the line of travel and the body turns sideways. First, the front feet respond by moving toward the side of the trail where the head is. Then, as the head turns more, the hind feet move to the side away from the head. The greater the head movement, the greater the angle of the side gait. Common examples are the side trot and side gallop often used by canids. These are often called a dog trot or dog gallop.

slow side trot / side gallop

An animal's size is also reflected in its gait patterns. When a mammal is walking with its normal gait, for example, the stride is 1.1 to 1.25 times larger than the distance from the hip to the shoulder joint. Using this crude relationship, body size can be judged from a walking stride. A 22-in stride

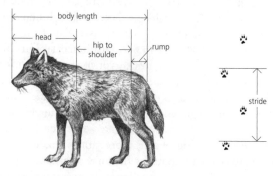

estimating mammal length from stride

indicates a hip-to-shoulder length of 20 in. Add to the hip-to-shoulder distance an estimate for the head length beyond the shoulder joint and an estimate of the rump length beyond the hip joint to get a total estimate of animal body length.

Speed also modifies gait patterns in trails. There are three rules governing how pattern changes as speed changes:

1. As speed increases, the hind foot lands farther forward than the front footprint on the same side. Conversely, as speed decreases, the hind foot lands farther back in relation to the front footprint.

2. As speed increases, stride increases.

3. As speed increases, straddle usually decreases.

walk
(slower)

amble
(faster)

front track large, hind small

| 1 x 2 x 1 lope | 2 x 2 lope | 3 x 3 lope |

Speed changes are easily observed in quadrupedal walk and trot trail patterns. As speed increases, the hind footprint registers in front of the front print. This faster version of a walk is called an amble. The faster version of a trot doesn't have a name. When the animal slows to the point that the hind feet are registering behind the front prints, the animal may be stalking something. Trots are separated from walks by having a stride two or more times greater than the estimated hip-to-shoulder distance of an animal.

A slow version of the gallop is also recognizable. When a gallop slows to the point that one or more hind feet register behind the leading edge of the frontmost footprint in a group pattern, the gait is called a *lope*. The gait is still a gallop, it's just a slow gallop.

Trail measurements

The terms *stride, group, intergroup,* and *straddle* describe the size of an animal trail. The stride is measured from the point where a foot touches the ground surface to where the same point of the same foot next touches the surface, and consists of one group and one intergroup measurement. The *group* consists of all four footprints (two fronts, two hinds, two lefts, two rights), while the *intergroup* is the distance between groups. Gait patterns take their name from the configuration of the group. The stride provides an indication of size in a walking animal and an indication of relative speed for other gaits (see pages xvii and xviii).

The *straddle* indicates the width of the trail and is measured from the outside rightmost pad of the outside right footprint of a group to the outside leftmost pad footprint of the same group. The outside edges of the trail are used because the inside of footprints overlap for many carnivore species.

Stride, group, and intergroup are all measured parallel to the trail, while the straddle is measured at right angles to the trail. Select a straight section of trail on level ground to measure. The slightest curve in the trail will distort the straddle measurement.

Glossary of terms

amble: a fast walk in which the hind footprint registers anterior to the front footprint. See illustration on page xviii.

asymmetrical: not symmetrical, that is, one side is not a mirror image of the opposite side.

bound: a gait in which both hind feet strike the ground at the same time, side by side. If the front feet also land side by side, the motion is said to be a full bound. A half bound occurs when one front foot strikes the ground in front of the other. See illustration on page xvi.

clout: term used to refer to toe 3 or toe 4 of the hoof. See illustration on page xxv.

convergent toes: Toes 2 and 4 of ducks, geese, and swans, which bend toward the foot axis, especially at the tips. Compare to divergent toes.

cord: See *scat shape*.

cough pellet: remnants of bones and hair coughed up by many bird species after feeding on prey.

dewclaw: toe that over evolutionary time has become reduced in size and raised on the leg, away from the other toes. For example, toe 1 in dogs and toes 2 and 5 in deer.

diagnostic: providing certain identification of an animal or its sign.

digitigrade: walking on the tips of the toes. Dogs and cats, for example, are digitigrade. Tracks left by digitigrade animals rarely show a sole. Compare *plantigrade*.

digit: one of the toes of an animal.

digital pad: See *pad*.

distal webbing: See *webbing*.

divergent toes: Toes that are straight or turn out from the *foot axis* at the tips, specifically toes 2 and 4 of sea gulls. Compare to *convergent toes*.

foot axis: imaginary line down the center of the foot. It runs between toes 3 and 4 in deer and their relatives, and down toe 3 of other mammals. In birds, the foot axis also runs down toe 3.

fringe: webbing attached to a single toe. May have a smooth edge, known as a simple fringe or simple lobe, or it may be wavy, in which case it is said to have indented lobes.

detached claw

indented lobe

detached toe

full bound: See *bound*.

gait: term for the type(s) of movement an animal uses when moving. Examples of gaits include walk, amble, trot, bound, and gallop. Gaits are defined by the mechanics of body movement, not by speed.

gallop: a gait in which hind feet move around the front feet and (usually) strike the ground in front of the front feet. Galloping forms distinct group patterns (two fronts, two hinds, two lefts, two rights) separated by an intergroup distance from the next set of four feet. Gallops fall into two basic patterns: Z-shaped and C-shaped.

group: a subunit of a stride including four footprints (two fronts and two hinds, and two lefts and two rights). The measure of the group plus the intergroup equals the measure of the stride.

half bound: See *bound*.

heel: portion of foot or track to the rear of digital and interdigital pads. In mammals, may be covered with hair, naked (without hair), or have one or more proximal pads. In reptiles and amphibians, may be textured with tubercles.

hop: synonymous with *bound,* often used in reference to gaits of rodents and rabbits.

indented lobe: See *fringe*.

interdigital pad: See *pad*.

length: of a track, the distance from front of toe pads to back of the interdigital pads, measured parallel to the foot axis. In mammal tracks, does not include claws. In bird tracks, does not include toe 1, but includes claws if they are attached and indistinguishable from toe pad.

line of travel: imaginary line on the ground over which the center of gravity of an animal passes.

lobe: See *fringe*.

lope: a slow gallop, in which at least one hind foot registers behind a front foot in a group of four footprints. See illustration on page xix.

mesial webbing: See *webbing*.

minimum outline: See pages xiii and xv for extended discussion.

nipple-dimple: See *scat shape*.

outer toe angle: in birds, the angle between toes 2 and 4. In perching birds it is less than 90 degrees, and in shorebirds it is greater than 120·.

oval: See *scat shape*.

pad: hard, callus-like structure on the sole of an animal's foot. Each toe may have a digital pad. One or more interdigital pads are located directly to the rear of the toes, and one or more proximal pads may be located directly to the rear of the interdigital pads. In deer and their relatives, there is a single pad separated from the wall by the subunguinis. In birds, a metatarsal pad may occur directly under the leg bone.

plantigrade: walking on the soles of the foot. Raccoons, bears, and humans, for example, are plantigrade. The sole of the foot usually shows in the footprint. Compare *digitigrade*.

pronk: a gait in which all four feet strike the ground simultaneously and directly below the body. The group pattern shows two front footprints ahead of the two hind prints. Also called a stot. See illustration on page xvii.

proximal pad: See *pad*.

proximal webbing: See *webbing*.

rotatory gallop: a type of gallop which tends to form a C-shaped group pattern. See illustration on page xvi.

run: a gait used when moving only on two legs. It differs from a walk by having a longer stride.

scat shape: Cords are long pieces of scat, typically four to ten times longer than the width. Ends may be blunt or tapered. Ovals are pieces of scat typically two to four times longer than wide and tapered at both ends. A "nipple-dimple" shaped scat pellet has a point at one end and a depression at the other. See chart on page xii.

simple fringe, simple lobe: See *fringe*.

sole: bottom of an animal's foot. It may be covered with hair or naked, and may have one or more pads on it.

stot: See *pronk*.

straddle: the distance from the right edge of the rightmost pad to the leftmost edge of the leftmost pad in a trail. Measured at right angles to the line of travel.

stride: The distance from the point where a foot touches the ground to the point where the same foot touches the ground again. Measured parallel to the line of travel. One stride is equal to a group plus an intergroup measurement.

subunguinis: the soft material under the nails of humans. In deer and their relatives, refers specifically to the soft material between the pad and wall.

symmetrical: having two sides, one the mirror image of the other side.

toe pad: See *pad*.

track: refers to an individual footprint. Some measurable characteristics include length and width.

track pattern: the gross visual image of the pattern of footprints on the ground. A repeating pattern of two prints separated from the next two is called "two-by" and written 2 x 2. Prints may also show patterns of 3 x 3, 4 x 4, and 1 x 2 x 1. These patterns are made during a gallop or a bound. A few of these patterns are illustrated on page xix.

trail: a series of footprints and associated sign that marks the passage of an animal. Some measurable characteristics include stride and straddle.

transverse gallop: a type of gallop which tends to form a Z-shaped group pattern. See illustration on page xvi.

trot: a gait in which evenly spaced footprints alternate on right and left sides of the line of travel. Hind footprint registers on top of front. As speed increases, hind moves forward of front. Same patterns as a walk, but longer stride. May be done with body turned to side. See illustration on page xvii.

tubercle: rough pinhead-sized protuberance on the sole of the foot of a reptile or amphibian.

fast
trot

unguinis: hard material forming nails in humans, hoof walls in deer and their relatives, and claws in other mammals. Composed of hair pasted together by body glues.

walk: a gait where evenly spaced footprints alternate on right and left sides of the line of travel. Hind footprint registers on top of front. As speed increases, hind moves forward of front. See illustrations on pages xvi and xviii.

wall: hard material around the edge of each clout of a hoof. Technically the unguinis, which also forms human nails and animal claws.

webbing: thin membrane stretched between toes of animals. The webbing may be near the tips of the toes (distal), about midway to the toe tips (mesial), or attached at the base (proximal). A membrane attached to only one toe is called a fringe.

width: of a track, the greatest distance from the right side of the pads of a foot to the left side, whether the greatest distance is across the toes or palm pads. Measured perpendicular to the foot axis. In bird tracks, includes claws if they are attached and indistinguishable from toe pad.

How to use *Scats and Tracks*

Scats and Tracks of the Rocky Mountains is designed for easy use in the field. The gray bars found on the edges of the pages of the track accounts will help you measure scat diameter and footprint size; each of these bars is keyed to the average size of the sign in question. A ruler is provided on the back cover. Below, I provide the background knowledge that every tracker should be familiar with before going to the field or using this book. Please take some time to study this material.

Illustrations

Illustrator Todd Telander applied his great ability to our collections of plaster casts, photographs, and slides, "drawing" on our experience to produce the most up-to-date and accurate illustrations possible. These drawings—made from the best specimens in a collection of thousands—represent the culmination of decades of tracking experience and are far more accurate than the tracker usually finds in tracking books. The tracks you find on the ground may not have as much detail or be as clear, but it is better to have an excellent drawing to compare to an imperfect track than to have to compare a track to a drawing lacking critical details.

How to use the track accounts

The track accounts in this guide have been grouped by similar footprint characteristics. Each track account represents a single species or a group of species with similar track characteristics. Each account is presented across a two-page spread, and is conveniently divided into sections as discussed below.

A brief listing of visual characteristics used to identify an animal begins each track account, appearing beneath the common and scientific names of the species. These descriptions are general, and great variability of pattern can exist among animals in the field. I recommend consulting appropriate field identification guides.

Track: A concise description of key points of footprints, to be used for identification. The accompanying track illustrations are not at actual size, but, unless otherwise noted, actual (average) length of the footprint is shown as a bar on the right side of the right-hand page. Average width is shown as a bar on the bottom of the right-hand page. In the field, place the appropriate measurement bar next to the track to compare size. To take a numerical measurement, use the ruler printed on the back cover of the book.

The tracks illustrated are all from right feet, except in the entries for birds, where both feet are pictured. Numerical measurements are given in the form *length x width*. Note that measurements of mammal tracks do not include claws, that measurements of bird tracks include claws but do not include toe 1, and that measurements generally do not include parts of the foot that often do not register in a given species's track (e.g., heels in the hind feet of some rodent species).

Trail: The average size of the stride of the most commonly used gait or gaits is given. Other common or characteristic gaits, if any, are discussed. See *track pattern* on page xxiv in the Glossary of Terms. For more information on gaits in tracking, see my *Field Guide to Mammal Tracking in North America*. Gaits are displayed up the right side of the right-hand page. If the common gait is a walk or trot, however, it may not be illustrated, since all walking and trotting patterns consist of right-left alternating patterns.

Scat: A description of scat supplements the drawing. Average scat width is shown as a bar up the side of the left-hand page. In the field, place the appropriate measurement bar next to the scat to compare sizes. To take a numerical measurement, use the ruler printed on the back cover of the book. Numerical measurements of scat are given under the illustrations in the form *length x width*. In cases of small scat, only width is given; thus, a single measurement always indicates diameter.

Habitat: To aid in locating and differentiating tracks, the animal's habitat preferences are listed. Some animals with large ranges, such as the beaver, are only found in specific habitats.

Similar species: Clues are provided to help differentiate an animal's tracks from similar tracks of other species. With these clues, identification should be possible.

Other sign: Other sign of animals, besides tracks and scat, are listed or illustrated to help with identification, and simply to provide more information on animal lives.

In addition, a distribution map is provided with each account. This gives a generalized picture of where in the

Rocky Mountains region an animal may be found. Animals that require specific habitats will of course not be evenly distributed through the shown range.

To make the best use of this guide, carry it with you into the field. When you come across an unfamiliar track or trail, open the book to the appropriate track account and place the page alongside the track for immediate on-site comparison.

Visual key to tracks

This simple key includes birds, reptiles, amphibians, and mammals. It is arranged by the number of toes that show in a good footprint, ranging from no toes to two toes to five toes. Those animals that show four toes in the front print and five toes in the hind are listed between four- and five-toed animals.

Snakes   (pp. 138–39)

Series of side-to-side trail undulations.

Deer and relatives   (pp. 82–99)

Two toes form hard, cloven hoof. Dewclaws may show in deep print.

Birds with webbed feet   (pp. 100–129)

Three toes facing forward, often a fourth toe facing backward. Claws may be detached from toes. Webbing between two or more toes.

Birds without webbed feet   (pp. 100–129)

Three toes facing forward, often a fourth toe facing backward. Claws may be detached from toes.

Wolves, dogs, and relatives (pp. 2–9)

Four toes in front and hind prints. Claws usually present and detached. Single anterior lobe on interdigital pad.

Cougars, cats, and relatives (pp. 10–15)

Four toes in front and hind prints. Claws usually absent. Double anterior lobe on interdigital pad.

Rabbits and relatives (pp. 16–23)

Four toes in front and hind footprint. An exceptionally clear print may show a fifth inner toe in the front footprint. Pads lacking, bottom of foot covered with hair. Long hopping heel in hind print.

Salamanders (pp. 130–31)

Four toes in front print, five toes in hind. Trail wide, often with a tail drag.

Frogs (pp. 134–37)

Four toes in front print, five toes in hind. Long, slender toes. Front print faces center of trail. Distal webbing in hind print.

Toads (pp. 132–33)

Four toes in front print, five toes in hind. Front print faces center of trail. Mesial webbing in hind print. Tubercles may show on front and hind prints.

Rodents (pp. 50–79)

Most have four toes in front prints and five in hind. Beaver has five toes in front print. Front toes show a 1-2-1 grouping, hind show a 1-3-1 grouping. Long hopping heel in hind print.

Lizards (pp. 140–141)

Five toes in front and hind prints. Toes long and slender. Claws may be detached. Tail drag often present in trail.

Turtles

Five toes show in front and hind tracks. Front prints toe-in and hind prints may toe-out. Feet are relatively broad. Claws robust and often visible. Sometimes the claws are the only visible signs on hard ground.

Opossum

Five toes. Distinct hind print with an opposable (like human thumb) inside toe protruding sideways from other toes. Outside toe is slightly separated from middle three toes.

Shrew (pp. 80–81)

Five slender toes present on front and hind feet. In clear prints, four interdigital and two proximal pads may be seen.

Raccoons and relatives (pp. 24–27)

Five toes in front and hind prints. Toes mostly round or bulbous at ends. May have long, slender toes.

Weasels and relatives (pp. 28–45)

Five toes in front and hind prints, though the little toe (on inside of foot) may not show. Toes in a 1-3-1 grouping. Interdigital pad is chevron-shaped. Plantigrade hind foot.

Black bear (pp. 48–49)

Five toes in front and hind prints, though the little toe (on inside of foot) may not show. Toes evenly spaced in a 1-3-1 grouping. Interdigital pad is chevron-shaped. Plantigrade hind foot.

Scats
and
Tracks
of the
Rocky Mountains

Gray Wolf
Canis lupus

Larger than a German shepherd, 110–130 lb (50–60 kg). Male larger than female. Color varies from completely black to gray to white. Short, rounded ears and short, wide, blocky muzzle.

Track: Track diameter of a grapefruit. Claws usually present; one lobe on leading edge of interdigital pad. Inside toe slightly larger than outside. Front foot larger than hind.

Trail: Trotting stride averages 62 in (155 cm). Often uses a C-shaped gallop or a trot with the body turned to the side, leaving a 2 x 2 pattern.

Scat: Varies from pure black, toothpaste-like animal protein to mostly hair with some bones. Tips tapered into long tails.

Habitat: Found in all habitats. Tends to use cover when possible, moving in forest or at forest-meadow edge.

Similar species: Track larger than other canids. At 60 days of age, track larger than adult coyote's. Differs from mountain lion by having one lobe on the leading edge of the interdigital pad

scat
4 x 1.25 in
10 x 3.2 cm

SCAT WIDTH

and usually showing claws. Differs from wolverine and bear by having only four toes, with the large toe on the inside.

Other sign: The alpha wolf, dominant member of the pack, marks its territory by urinating on raised objects along the trail. Blood observed during January or February in the female's urine stain may indicate readiness to breed. Scratch marks beside urine stains or scat are territorial markings, and are usually made with hind feet.

urine mark of alpha wolf

side trot

front
4.25 x 4 in
10.7 x 10 cm

hind
3.75 x 3.25 in
9.5 x 8.2 cm

gallop

FRONT TRACK LENGTH

FRONT TRACK WIDTH

Coyote
Canis latrans

Collie-sized canid, 20–25 lb (9–11 kg). Male larger than female. Color varies from completely gray to tan to rust. Long, pointed ears and long, narrow muzzle.

Track: Claws usually present, one lobe on the leading edge of the interdigital pad. Inside toe slightly larger than outside. Front foot larger than hind.

Trail: Trotting stride averages 39 in (100 cm). Often uses a trot with body turned to the side, leaving a 2 x 2 track pattern. Often lopes, leaving a C-shaped pattern.

Scat: Varies from pure black animal protein to mostly hair with some bones. Tips tapered into long tails.

Habitat: An animal of the open brush country, the coyote digs its den on exposed hilltops or ridges with a view of surrounding area. Where persecuted, may den in a more secluded location.

Similar species: Even adult track is smaller than that of a wolf pup. Track may overlap in size with that of red fox, but lacks

scat
3 x 0.6 in
7.5 x 1.5 cm

SCAT WIDTH

callus ridge of red fox. Track larger than gray fox, and usually shows claws. Differs from bobcat by showing claws and by having one lobe on leading edge of interdigital pad.

Other sign: Marks territory with urine and scat piles. Scat pile locations may be used repeatedly. Uses feet to scratch near scat piles, spreading odor from scat and feet glands to identify territory.

scratch marks near scat pile

front
2.5 x 2.35 in
6.3 x 5.8 cm

hind
2.25 x 1.9 in
5.7 x 4.8 cm

lope

side trot

FRONT TRACK LENGTH

FRONT TRACK WIDTH

Red Fox
Vulpes vulpes

Border collie–
sized, 6–15 lb
(3–7 kg).
Reddish
yellow with
black stockings
and a white tip
on the tail.
Regional color phases include silver, black, cross, and bluish
gray. Long, pointed ears and elongate, pointed muzzle.

Track: Claws prominent. A ridge of callus present across interdigital pad. One lobe on the leading edge of the interdigital pad. Inside toe slightly larger than outside. Front foot larger than hind.

Trail: Trotting stride averages 32 in (80 cm). Typically uses a trotting gait and, occasionally, a 2 x 2 trot with body turned to the side. Walks more than coyote, especially in shrubs.

Scat: Often has tapered tail. Composition varies. Mouse or rabbit fur, berries, and insects are common. Bird feathers and plant remains often present.

Habitat: Found in a variety of habitats from brush to croplands to mixed hard- and softwood forest. Prefers edges, where hunting

scat
2 x 0.6 in
5 x 1.5 cm

log

for small mammals is good. Also found in urban areas, where may find cover during the daytime. Not found in dense forests.

Similar species: Differs from other canids by having a ridge of callus on the interdigital pad. Track tends to be larger than gray fox, and usually shows claws. Differs from bobcat in having only one lobe on the interdigital pad and claws (usually) showing.

Other sign: Multiple dens are used each season. Often digs own den. A given den may be used for several years. Look for small bones around den entrance. Scat has a diagnostic musky odor, produced by a musk gland on the top of the tail. Learn to identify this unique "foxy" odor. Foxes tight-rope walk on narrow logs.

side trot

front
2 x 1.8 in
5 x 4.5 cm

hind
1.9 x 1.7 in
4.8 x 4.3 cm

trot

FRONT TRACK LENGTH

FRONT TRACK WIDTH

Gray Fox
Urocyon cinereoargenteus

Smaller than a border collie, 8–11 lb (4–5 kg). Body color is pepper-and-salt. A black stripe runs down the back and upper side of tail. Sides are reddish. Tip of tail is black. Long, pointed ears and elongate, pointed muzzle.

Track: Small for a canid, somewhat broad and therefore somewhat cat-like. Claws, rarely present in track, are very small and sharp, giving the gray fox the ability to climb trees like a cat. Front foot larger than hind.

Trail: Generally a trot. Trotting stride averages 24 in (60 cm). Walks more than coyote.

Scat: Often has tapered tail. Composition varies, as the gray fox is opportunistic when feeding. Rabbit fur is most common, followed by fur of other small mammals, berries, and insects. Plant remains are often present.

scat
2 x 0.6 in
5 x 1.5 cm

Habitat: Prefers a mixture of fields and woods. More often found in woodlands than are red fox. Early stage woodlands are preferred, with considerable activity in riparian habitats.

Similar species: Smaller than coyote and wolf. Lacks the ridge of callus on the interdigital pad of the red fox. Differs from coyote in that claws often do not show.

side trot

Other sign: Seldom digs dens, but makes use of woodpiles, rock outcrops, hollow trees, and brushpiles. Look for small bones around den entrances.

climbing tree

front
1.8 x 1.6 in
4.5 x 4.0 cm

hind
1.7 x 1.6 in
4.3 x 4.0 cm

trot

FRONT TRACK LENGTH

FRONT TRACK WIDTH

Mountain Lion
Puma concolor

Larger than a German shepherd, with male averaging 145 lb (66 kg) and female about 120 lb (54 kg). Color gray to red, often called "tawny," with whitish underside. Back of ears and tip of tail black to brown. Tail is over half the length of the body. Also called cougar or puma.

Track: Track diameter of a baseball. Front tracks round or wider than long, and hind tracks longer than wide. Claw impressions are usually absent. Toes form a slight arc and toe 3 leads. Leading edge of the interdigital pad has two lobes. Inside toe distinctly larger.

Trail: Walking stride is about 36 in (90 cm). Usually walks, but bounds with hind feet placed side by side when chasing prey.

Scat: Scat from a fresh kill may form a uniform diameter cord with very slight constrictions; ends usually blunt. As the carcass a lion is feeding on dries out, the lion's scat tends to develop constrictions, eventually falling apart when diet becomes very dry.

scat
4 x 1.25 in
10 x 3.2 cm

SCAT WIDTH

Habitat: Habitat is that of its main prey, deer. Open woodlands with rock ledges and grass (for deer) preferred. Often found in riparian zones with trees.

Similar species: Track differs from wolf by the presence of two lobes on the leading edge of the interdigital pad, by having toe 3 leading, and by usually not showing claws. Differs from wolverine and bears by having only four toes.

Other sign: Often buries scat by scraping dirt over it with front feet. Scraped ground material may conceal food caches. Male will rake up basketball-sized patches of brush and urinate on them to mark home range.

bound

scraped ground around scat

two lobes

front
3.5 x 3.6 in
8.8 x 9.0 cm

hind
3.25 x 3 in
8.2 x 7.5 cm

walk

FRONT TRACK LENGTH

FRONT TRACK WIDTH

Canada Lynx

Felis lynx

Larger than a collie, with male averaging about 22 lb (10 kg) and female 19 lb (9 kg). Very long legs and big feet. Reddish to yellowish brown overall, with dark spots or streaks and whitish underside. Ears have tufts at tips. Tail tip is black on top and bottom. Tail is short or "bobbed," about 4 in (10 cm) long.

Track: Diameter of a softball and indistinct because the feet are mostly covered with hair, and because pads are reduced in size. Feet are large, for better support on snow.

Trail: Walking stride is about 28 in (72 cm). Walking gaits are common, but lynx does trot more than bobcat. Winter trails often show random vertical leaps, perhaps signalling that the lynx has jumped after a flying bird.

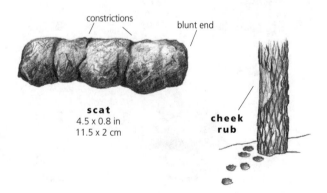

constrictions

blunt end

scat
4.5 x 0.8 in
11.5 x 2 cm

cheek rub

Scat: Tends to be constricted and, if dry, separates at constrictions into segments. Ends blunt. Dry scat falls apart. Scat from a fresh kill may form a uniform diameter cord.

Habitat: Found in dense conifer forests interspersed with rocky ledges and downed timber, both of which are used for security and denning. Forest edges, which provide food for the lynx's major prey, snowshoe hare, are critical.

Similar species: Track differs from other felids by being inherently indistinct. Interdigital pad is relatively small when compared to bobcat and mountain lion—check closely.

Other sign: Birth dens occur in hollow logs, stumps, and clumps of timber. Adult lynx does not cover scat. Lynx urinates (scent marks) up to 25 times per mile.

fast trot

vertical leap from hind feet

trot

walk

front
4 x 3.8 in
10 x 9.5 cm

small hairless pads

small interdigital pads

hind
3.75 x 4.1 in
9.5 x 10.3 cm

FRONT TRACK LENGTH

FRONT TRACK WIDTH

Bobcat
Felis rufus

Size of a collie, with male averaging about 17 lb (8 kg) and female 13 lb (6 kg). Overall color reddish to yellowish brown, with dark spots or streaks and whitish underside. Ears have tufts at tips. Back of ears and top of tail tip black. Tail is short or "bobbed," about 4 in (10cm) long.

Track: Front tracks are round or wider than long. Hind tracks may be longer than wide. Claw impressions are usually absent. Toes form a slight arc and toe 3 leads. The leading edge of the interdigital pad has two lobes. Inside toe distinctly larger than outside toe.

Trail: Walking stride is about 20 in (50 cm). Usually walks, but bounds with hind feet placed side-by-side when chasing prey.

Scat: Tends to be constricted and, if dry, separates at constrictions into segments. Ends usually blunt. Dry scat falls apart. Scat from a fresh kill may form a uniform diameter cord.

broken constriction

scat
3 x 0.8 in
7.5 x 2 cm

Habitat: Prefers dense cover of swamps and forests, especially with rocky ledges. Open agricultural land is not used. Rock piles, caves, and high rocky ledges are important for bearing young.

Similar species: Differs from coyote by lacking claws, having two lobes on the leading edge of the interdigital pad, and having toe 3 leading. Substantially smaller than both lion and lynx.

Other sign: Scent marks made by urine, scat, and anal glands. Scrapes dirt or snow over urine and scat. Scratches from rubbing glands are apparent on snow. Caches food by burying.

walk

vertical leap from hind feet

bound

walk

leading toe

two lobes

front
2 x 2.1 in
5 x 5.3 cm

claw marks on tree

hind
2.1 x 1.9 in
5.3 x 4.8 cm

FRONT TRACK LENGTH

FRONT TRACK WIDTH

Jack Rabbit

Lepus species

White-tailed jack rabbit
L. townsendii

Large, slender hare
with long ears and
feet. Averages about
5 lb (2 kg). Body color
is gray and white to
black and white.
Black-tailed jack
rabbit *(L. californicus)*
is smaller, with black
tail. White-tailed jack rabbit *(L. townsendii)* has white tail, and
may turn white in the winter.

Track: Toes asymmetrical around foot axis.
Track indistinct because foot is completely
haired and lacks pads. Occasionally claws
will register, and may be the only sign of
a footprint. Hind footprint may be up to
three times longer than front. Hind print
of white-tailed jack rabbit averages about
10 percent longer than black-tailed.

Trail: Galloping stride may reach 10 feet
(300 cm). Tends to gallop rather than bound.

Scat: Dry scat is a slightly flattened sphere. Produces a black,
semiliquid scat that is usually reingested to utilize remaining
nutrients.

scat
0.3 in
0.8 cm

Habitat: Inhabits open areas. Black-tailed is found in arid regions with sparse grass and desert vegetation. White-tailed is found from plains grasslands to above tree line in the mountains.

Similar species: Track differs from cottontail by having long shape. Differs from snowshoe hare by its narrow width.

Other sign: Sharp incisors cleanly cut herbaceous and woody vegetation. The jack rabbit's nest, known as a **form,** is a shallow depression, usually found under protective cover.

sharp cut grass

toe position asymmetrical

front
1.7 x 1.4 in
4.3 x 3.5 cm

hind
5 x 1.5 in
12.5 x 3.8 cm

gallop

FRONT TRACK LENGTH

FRONT TRACK WIDTH

Snowshoe Hare

Lepus americanus

Medium-sized hare with long
ears and feet. Averages about
3 lb (1.4 kg). Body color is
rusty to gray brown, turning
white in the winter. Ears retain
their black tip in winter.

Track: Toes asymmetrical around
foot axis. Track indistinct because
the foot is completely haired and
lacks pads. Hind footprint may be up to
two and a half times longer than front.
To provide flotation on snow, hind feet
are exceptionally wide and toes may splay
apart so that width approaches length.

Trail: Hopping stride varies from 3–6 ft
(90–180 cm). Tends to hop with paired
hind feet.

Scat: Dry scat is a slightly flattened sphere. Produces a black,
semiliquid scat that is usually reingested to utilize remaining
nutrients.

scat
0.3 in
0.8 cm

**chewed
branch and
cone**

SCAT WIDTH

Habitat: High mountains with deep snows. Dense second-growth forest is preferred, but swamps are also used. Forages at forest edge and in small clearings.

Similar species: Track differs from cottontail by its large size and from jack rabbit by its relative width.

Other sign: Look for woody plants, including conifers, that have had the tips of branches chewed off. During population highs, hares will strip tree bark and have been observed feeding on carcasses. The snowshoe's nest, a shallow depression known as a **form,** is found under conifer branches or logs.

toe position asymmetrical

front
1.75 x 1.5 in
4.4 x 3.8 cm

hind
4.5 x 3.75 to 4.5 in
12.5 x 9.4 to 12.5 cm

hop

FRONT TRACK LENGTH

FRONT TRACK WIDTH

Cottontail Rabbit

Sylvilagus spp.

Small rabbit with large ears and feet, but small white tail. Averages about 1 lb (0.5 kg). Color pepper-and-salt or gray and white. Several species of cottontail are found in the region. While the tracks of these species are indistinguishable from one another, tracks may vary in size.

Mountain Cottontail
S. nuttalii

Track: Toes asymmetrical around foot axis. Track indistinct because the foot is completely haired and lacks pads. Occasionally claws will register; these may be the only sign of a hopping rabbit. Hind footprint about two and a half times longer than front.

Trail: Hopping stride is about 3 ft (90 cm). Most of the time rabbits hop, but walking patterns will occasionally be observed.

Scat: Dry scat is a slightly flattened sphere. Produces a black, semiliquid scat that is usually reingested to utilize remaining nutrients.

scat
0.2 in
0.5 cm

chewed branch and bud

SCAT WIDTH

Habitat: Found wherever there is grass for food and suitable cover, including brushpiles, herbaceous and shrubby vegetation, and grasslands. May use dens of other animals for escape cover.

Similar species: Differs from jack rabbit and hare by having shorter heels and smaller overall size.

Other sign: Sharp incisors cleanly cut herbaceous vegetation at the height of a sitting rabbit 4–8 in (10–20 cm). Look for tips of branches with young sprouts chewed off. The cottontail's bed, known as a **form,** is a shallow depression in earth, grass, or snow.

walk

claws only on hard ground

hop

claw

toe position asymmetrical

front
1.25 x 1 in
3.2 x 2.5 cm

hind
3.5 x 1 in
8.8 x 2.5 cm

FRONT TRACK LENGTH

FRONT TRACK WIDTH

Pika
Ochotona princeps

Small (average weight 5 oz/140 g), rat-sized, short-legged, nearly tailless, egg-shaped member of the rabbit order (Lagomorpha). Large ears and relatively large eyes. Color gray to grayish brown.

Track: Shows four toes. Only in a very clear footprint will the minute inside toe on the front foot be observed. Unlike the rest of the rabbit order, the pika's track shows toe pads. The sole is haired.

Trail: Prefers a hop, with a stride of 15 in (38 cm). Even when moving fast, the stride is seldom more than three times the group.

Scat: Produces two types of scat. The most readily found are nearly spherical and dry. Also produces a black, semiliquid scat that is usually reingested to utilize remaining nutrients.

scat
0.1 in
0.3 cm

SCAT WIDTH

Habitat: Found almost exclusively in the rock and talus fields of high mountains.

Similar species: Differs from chipmunk and other rodents by having only four toes on hind foot. Track is larger than mouse or vole.

Other sign: Marks territory by urinating on prominent rocks, leaving a white, hard stain. Scat may be placed nearby. Stores plants under and around rocks near the center of its territory. These hay piles dry and provide food for the pika during the winter.

hay pile

front
0.75 x 0.6 in
1.9 x 1.5 cm

minute inside toe

hind
1 x 0.75 in
2.5 x 1.9 cm

hop

FRONT TRACK LENGTH

FRONT TRACK WIDTH

Raccoon
Procyon lotor

Stocky, smaller than a collie, with broad head and bushy tail. Male averages about 18 lb (8 kg) and female about 16 lb (7 kg). Gray to black overall, with black rings on the tail and a black mask on a white face.

Track: Five slender toes, slightly bulbous on the ends. Feet resemble small human hands and feet. Hind foot has a long, naked heel.

Trail: Walking stride averages 27 in (70 cm). Roll of hips during walk causes hind foot to register beside the opposite front print. C-shaped gallop is common.

Scat: Highly variable, but often black, even-diameter cord with blunt ends. Often contains crayfish or fruit. Deposited singly or in dung heaps containing scat from perhaps several individuals. May carry a parasite that is fatal to humans. Do not smell scat, and wash hands after touching.

Habitat: River and stream drainages are prime habitats, but storm drains in cities may also provide refuge.

blunt end

scat
3 x 0.75 in
7.5 x 1.9 cm

SCAT WIDTH

Similar species: Differs from bear in having slender toes. Differs from river otter by lack of webbing. Larger than mink.

Other sign: Digs holes in stream banks to get at crayfish. Leaves piles of crayfish skeletons and claws. Digs for worms in lawns.

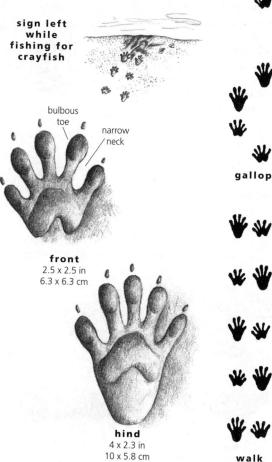

sign left while fishing for crayfish

bulbous toe

narrow neck

front
2.5 x 2.5 in
6.3 x 6.3 cm

hind
4 x 2.3 in
10 x 5.8 cm

gallop

walk

FRONT TRACK LENGTH

FRONT TRACK WIDTH

Ringtail

Bassariscus astutus

Small, rat-sized, with a bushy tail as long as its body. Males average about 1.5–2.5 lb (0.7–1.1 kg), with females slightly smaller. Pointed face, large eyes and ears. Tan to gray overall, with some black hairs. Tail has black bands alternating with white to a black tip.

Track: Five toes, round and somewhat bulbous, with an extra proximal pad showing in the front print. Claws are semi-retractile and may not show.

Trail: Bounding stride is 12–16 in (30–40 cm). Uses a relatively slow bound or lope much of the time.

Scat: Usually composed of plant material, but occasionally black animal protein scats are found. Insects and fruits are often present.

scat
2 x 0.4 in
5 x 1 cm

chewed cactus on cliff runway

SCAT WIDTH

Habitat: Found in a variety of habitats from riparian to desert to open woodland to evergreen forest. Rest sites and dens are located in rocks, burrows, brushpiles, and hollow limbs. Not adverse to using buildings for nests and dens.

Similar species: Differs from domestic cats, bobcats, and small foxes by having five toes and an extra proximal pad.

Other sign: Runways at the base of cliffs are used repeatedly and trails often lead to a single rock crevice where it dens.

lope

proximal pad

front
1 x 1 in
2.5 x 2.5 cm

hind
1 x 1 in
2.5 x 2.5 cm

bound

FRONT TRACK LENGTH

Wolverine

Gulo gulo

Body like a badger's,
but heavier, up to
35 lb (16 kg). Male
larger than female.
Head broad, rounded,
and flat. Color varies from overall dark brown with light
blond side stripes to nearly all blond. Short tail.

Track: Track diameter of a baseball. Five toes, in 1-3-1 grouping. Little toe, on the inside of foot, sometimes does not register. Interdigital pad is a chevron. Proximal pad and heel often show. Distinct winter tracks because feet are not well furred.

Trail: Gallop stride averages 35 in (90 cm). Mostly 2 x 2 and 3 x 3 gallop patterns.

Scat: Long, medium-diameter cord occasionally folding back on itself. Black or brown, occasionally with hair. Tapered at both ends. Similar to large coyote scat.

Habitat: Not habitat-specific. Wanders widely in all seasons, though often found where there are wintering deer, elk, or moose.

tail

scat
4 x 0.5 in
10 x 1.3 cm

**raided
kill trap**

SCAT WIDTH

Similar species: Larger than mink, marten, and fisher, and only rarely climbs trees. Differs from wolf and lion by having five toes. Differs from bear by having 1-3-1 toe grouping and chevron-shaped interdigital pad.

Other sign: Scavenges on old carcasses, including those of animals caught in kill traps. Revisits sites to dig carcasses from under snow. Drags stomach over objects that protrude from ground or snow to scent mark, leaving scratches. Trails cross large openings in trees and are often found above tree line. Travels on packed trails and roads.

3 x 3 gallop

1 x 2 x 1 gallop

proximal pad

front
3.7 x 3.8 in
9.1 x 9.4 cm

naked heel

hind
4 x 3.5 in
9.9 x 8.8 cm

FRONT TRACK LENGTH

FRONT TRACK WIDTH

River Otter
Lutra canadensis

Body and tail form a
four-foot-long cylinder
that tapers to a hairy,
pointed tail. Weight varies
from 10–30 lb (5–14 kg).
Male slightly larger than female.
Overall color is a rich, dark brown, with silver-brown belly.
Webbed toes on front and hind feet.

Track: Large webbed foot is diagnostic, but look closely because webbing may be difficult to see. Hind foot is very wide. Five toes, in 1-3-1 grouping. Little toe, on the inside of foot, sometimes does not register. Interdigital pad is a chevron. Proximal pad often shows. Hairless heel on hind foot.

Trail: Walking stride averages 19 in (48 cm). Loping stride averages 32 in (80 cm). Loping gait patterns are usually turned to the side.

Scat: Usually contains fish remains, including scales and vertebrae. The texture is oily and the smell fishy. Fish oil keeps scat composed of fish scales from falling apart. Scat decomposes as oil evaporates, eventually falling into a pile of scales.

fish parts ——

scat
5 x 1 in
12.5 x 2.5 cm

Habitat: River and stream beds. Lives and nests in bank burrows, but may also nest in log jams. In spring, travels overland, often several miles from water sources.

Similar species: Differs from other species by webbing and wide hind foot.

Other sign: Loose dirt banks show where otters have rolled to dry off. Rolls around tufts of grass, twisting them into scent posts. Travels by sliding down banks, and along level snow and over ice-covered lakes.

tail drag

side lope

webbing

proximal
pad

front
2.5 x 3 in
6.3 x 7.5 cm

web

hind
3 x 3.6 in
7.5 x 9 cm

bound

FRONT TRACK LENGTH

FRONT TRACK WIDTH

Badger

Taxidea taxus

Border collie–sized with flat body, long hair, and long, shovel-like claws, about 18 lb (8 kg). Male 25 percent larger than female.

Color varies from silver-gray to yellowish brown on back. Belly white. Feet are black or dark brown. White stripe down nose with black markings on sides of face. Short tail.

Track: Diameter of a golf ball, with long front claws, nearly as long as footprint. Five toes, in 1-3-1 grouping. Little toe, on the inside of foot, sometimes does not register. Interdigital pad is a chevron. Proximal pad often shows. Front footprint larger than hind.

Trail: Walking stride averages 14 in (36 cm). Walking is most common, but trotting, with a stride of 29 in (74 cm), occurs frequently.

Scat: Seldom found because deposited below ground in burrows. Similar to, but smaller than, coyote scat, without tapered ends.

blunt ends

scat
3 x 0.8 in
7.5 x 2 cm

hole with dirt mound

Habitat: Open grasslands preferred. Areas with large populations of prey, which includes ground squirrels and prairie dogs.

Similar species: Differs from all other species by long claws on front foot and disproportionately small hind foot.

Other sign: Fresh excavations of large amounts of dirt from burrowing rodent holes indicates hunting activity, especially if excavated material includes large clods or rocks. Freshly widened burrow entrances may have a slightly elliptical shape. The presence of coyote and badger tracks together indicates cooperative hunting.

long, prominent claws

proximal pad

front
2.5 x 2 in
6.3 x 5 cm

heel not included in track measurement

hind
1.75 x 1.75 in
4.5 x 4.5 cm

lope

walk

FRONT TRACK LENGTH

FRONT TRACK WIDTH

Fisher

Martes pennanti

Larger than a
large house cat,
but slender, 7.5–
12 lb (3–5 kg).
Male larger than
female. Pointed, flat skull with small ears. Color is dark
brown. Long bushy tail.

Track: Five toes, in 1-3-1 grouping. Little
toe, on the inside of foot, sometimes does
not register. Interdigital pad is a chevron. Proximal pad may show in front footprint. Heel seldom shows. Claws short.
Feet are not well furred, which, in winter, makes toes appear clearly in tracks.

Trail: Gallop stride averages 28 in (71 cm).
Mostly gallops, but walking, 3 x 3, and
4 x 4 gallop patterns are also common.

Scat: Only mustelid scat that frequently contains porcupine quills.
Long, slender cord, usually tending to fold back on itself. Black
or brown in color, occasionally with hair. Tapered at both ends.

Habitat: Old-growth forest, especially among conifers and large
timber, and in swamp areas. Will use young forest stands following

folded back

tail

scat
3.5 x 0.5 in
8.8 x 1.3 cm

SCAT WIDTH

fire or timber harvest. Avoids open areas without overhead cover, but will travel on roads and trails.

Similar species: Lacks the webbed toes of the mink. Differs from mink by habitat and use of terrestrial sites. Larger than mink and marten and occupies areas of shallower snow. Smaller than wolverine and makes more frequent use of trees for walkways and nests.

Other sign: Porcupine skins turned inside out. Snow trails may reveal frequent trips up trees. Walks on logs to avoid deep snow. Drags stomach over objects that protrude from the ground or snow to scent mark, leaving scratches. Travels on packed trails of snowshoe hare.

1 x 2 x 1 lope

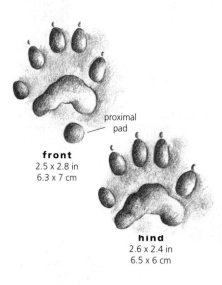

proximal pad

front
2.5 x 2.8 in
6.3 x 7 cm

hind
2.6 x 2.4 in
6.5 x 6 cm

3 x 3 lope

2 x2 gallop

FRONT TRACK LENGTH

FRONT TRACK WIDTH

Striped Skunk

Mephitis mephitis

Black-and-white mustelid, size of a domestic cat, with triangular head. Weight varies from 4–10 lb (2–5 kg).

Male is slightly larger than female. Flat, wide, bushy tail with white hair on top. Long, curved claws for digging.

Track: Half dollar–sized, with long front claws. Hind track looks like a little human footprint. Five toes, in 1-3-1 grouping. Little toe, on the inside of foot, sometimes does not register. Interdigital pad is a chevron. Proximal pad often shows. Hairless heel on hind foot.

Trail: Walking stride averages 12 in (30 cm). Meanders and stops often when walking, leaving "extra footprints" in trail. Lope may be turned to the side or straight forward.

Scat: Cylindrical with blunt ends. Lacks the long taper and tendency to fold back on itself of other mustelid scat. May be composed entirely of insect parts.

blunt

scat
5 x 0.75 in
12.5 x 1.9 cm

chewed eggs

SCAT WIDTH

Habitat: Not habitat-specific. Lives where burrows, cavities, or tunnels are present, including in and around buildings. Presence of insects and small mammals is critical to habitat selection.

Similar species: Differs from other species by having long, wide claws on the front foot. Smaller than badger, with front and hind feet similar in size.

Other sign: Smell of skunk musk identifies nests and burrows. Tears apart nests of small mammals. Bird eggs show four fang punctures around larger hole in shell.

insect remains

lope

long wide claws

proximal pad

front
1.5 x 1.25 in
3.8 x 3.1 cm

hind
1.9 x 1.4 in
4.8 x 3.5 cm

side lope

Mink

Mustela vison

Size of a small
domestic cat, but
slender, 1.5–3.5 lb
(0.7–1.5 kg). Male 10
percent larger than
female. Pointed, flat
skull with small ears.

Overall color is dark brown, with white spots on chin and
chest. Hairy, slender tail. Webbing occurs between the toes.

Track: Five toes, in 1-3-1 grouping. Little
toe, on the inside of foot, sometimes does
not register. Webbing shows between toes
in tracks; look carefully. Interdigital pad
is a chevron. Proximal pad may show in
front footprint. Heel seldom shows.

Trail: Bounding stride averages 14 in
(35 cm). Bounds more than weasels, but
a gallop, averaging 20 in (50 cm), is also
common.

Scat: Long, slender cord, usually tending to fold back on itself.
Black or brown in color, occasionally with hair. Tapered at both
ends. Often contains remains of fish or crayfish. May be oily
and smell fishy. Fish oil keeps scat composed of fish scales from
falling apart until oil evaporates, then scales scatter on the ground.

tail

folded back

fish bones

scat
2 x 0.25 in
5 x 0.6 cm

Habitat: River and stream banks. Seldom far from water.

Similar species: Differs from other small mustelids by having more webbing between toes. Larger than weasels. Use of aquatic habitat is an important clue for separation from marten. Tracks and trail much smaller than otter's.

Other sign: Mink make "post offices," repeated scat deposits on logs exposed above water's edge. Strong, musky, almost skunk-like odor from anal scent glands.

fast walk

front
1.7 x 1.8 in
4.2 x 4.4 cm

hind
1.8 x 1.9 in
4.5 x 4.8 cm

bound

FRONT TRACK LENGTH

FRONT TRACK WIDTH

Black-footed Ferret

Mustela nigripes

Long and slender, twice the size of a weasel. Weighs 1.4–3 lb (0.6–1.4 kg). Pointed, flat skull with small ears. Overall color pale yellow-brown, with dark hairs on back. Black mask across the eyes. Black feet and tail tip. Hairy, slender tail.

Track: Five toes, in 1-3-1 grouping. Little toe, on the inside of foot, sometimes does not register. Interdigital pad is a chevron. Proximal pad may show in front footprint. Heel may show. Claws may not show.

Trail: Galloping and bounding strides average 20 in (50 cm). Bounds more than weasels, but a gallop is very common.

Scat: Long, slender cord, usually with black, toothpaste-like animal protein or hair. Cord tends to fold back on itself. Tapered at both ends.

Habitat: Found in prairie dog towns in native short-grass prairies (prairie dogs are their main food).

folded back

tail

scat
2.25 x 0.25 in
5.6 x 0.6 cm

Similar species: Differs from weasel by larger track and trail. Differs from mink and marten by (sometimes) being larger. Mink and marten are seldom found in prairie dog towns.

Other sign: Excavated subsoil trough extending 40–55 in (100–140 cm) from prairie dog mounds.

3 x 3 gallop

trough

proximal pad

front
1.2 x 1.3 in
3 x 3.3 cm

4 x 4 gallop

heel not included in track measurement

hind
1.3 x 1.3 in
3.3 x 3.3 cm

2 x 2 bound

FRONT TRACK LENGTH

FRONT TRACK WIDTH

Marten

Martes americana

Size of a small house cat, but slender, 1–2 lb (0.5–1 kg). Male 20 percent larger than female. Pointed, flat skull with small ears. Overall color golden brown, with orange to yellow chest patch. Edges of ears are white. Hairy, slender tail.

Track: Five toes, in 1-3-1 grouping. Little toe, on the inside of foot, sometimes does not register. Interdigital pad is a chevron. Proximal pad may show in front footprint. Heel often shows. Feet are well furred in winter, making tracks indistinct.

Trail: Gallop stride averages 22 in (55 cm). Mostly gallops; a variety of 2 x 2, 3 x 3, and 4 x 4 patterns will be found.

Scat: Long, slender cord, tending to fold back on itself. Black or brown in color, occasionally with hair. Tapered at both ends.

Habitat: Old-growth forest, but adaptable to many forest habitats. Prefers mature conifer and mixed forests. Needs tall, hollow, or

scat
2 x 0.25 in
5 x 0.6 cm

folded back

SCAT WIDTH

climbs tree, jumps out

broken trees for denning. Found near its prey, squirrels and red-backed voles.

Similar species: Differs from weasel by its larger size. Lacks the webbed toes of the mink. Also differs from mink by use of terrestrial habitat. Smaller than fisher and occupies areas with deeper snow.

Other sign: Frequently burrows beneath snow and climbs up trees; look for tracks that end at a tree trunk. Scratch marks show where stomach was dragged over objects that protrude from the ground or snow to scent mark.

4 x 4 gallop

proximal pad

front
2.1 x 2 in
5.3 x 5 cm

furred heel, not
included in track
measurement

hind
2.3 x 2.1 in
5.8 x 5.3 cm

2 x 2 gallop

FRONT TRACK LENGTH

FRONT TRACK WIDTH

Weasels
Mustela spp.

Long-tailed weasel
M. frenata

Three species
with long,
slender bodies,
varying in size
from a regular to a foot-long hotdog. Pointed, flat skull
with small ears. Males are up to twice as large as females.
Largest males are about 1 lb (0.5 kg). Overall color is brown,
with a white belly. In winter, northern individuals turn
entirely white. Hairy, slender tail. The small least weasel
(M. nivalis) lacks the black tip on the tail found in the ermine
(M. erminea) and the long-tailed weasel *(M. frenata)*.

Track: Wide track. Five toes, in 1-3-1 grouping. Little toe, on inside of foot, often does not register. Interdigital pad is a chevron. Heel seldom shows. Difficult to distinguish between species.

Trail: Galloping stride varies from 8–30 in (20–75 cm). Side-by-side tracks, when examined closely, show one track slightly in front of the other—a gallop. In snow, a drag mark may be found between front and hind prints, sometimes forming a dumbbell shape.

Scat: Long, slender cord, usually with black, toothpaste-like animal protein or hair. Cord tends to fold back on itself. Tapered at both ends.

folded back

scat
1.5 x 0.1 in
3.8 x 0.3 cm

tail

SCAT WIDTH

Habitat: Prefer dense, low ground cover to open areas. Found in habitats where their prey, rodents, occur in high densities. Trails often lead from one rodent den to another. Travel in snow and ground burrows of other mammals.

Similar species: Differ from other mustelids by their smaller size and the drag mark commonly located between twin track patterns in the snow.

Other sign: Routes seldom follow a straight line; often have many sharp turns. Scat often deposited on raised objects.

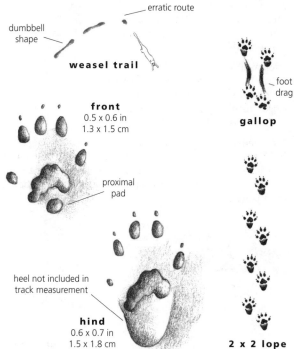

erratic route

dumbbell shape

weasel trail

front
0.5 x 0.6 in
1.3 x 1.5 cm

proximal pad

heel not included in track measurement

hind
0.6 x 0.7 in
1.5 x 1.8 cm

foot drag

gallop

2 x 2 lope

FRONT TRACK LENGTH

FRONT TRACK WIDTH

Grizzly Bear
Ursus arctos horribilis

Large, cow-sized bear, female averaging about 350 lb (160 kg) and male about 450 lb (200 kg). Both sexes have hump over shoulders. Color varies from black to brown to blond. Light tips on individual hairs create the grizzled appearance for which grizzlies are named.

Track: Claws on front foot, typically more than 1.5 times longer than toes. Webbing occurs between toes; look carefully. Hind print has a large, human-like heel. Outside toe larger than others.

Trail: Walking stride is 50–60 in (125–150 cm). Usually ambles, a fast walk where the hind foot oversteps the front. Gait is pigeon-toed. Lopes in a C-shaped pattern or uses a side gallop.

Scat: Normally contains vegetation and is sweet-smelling. When feeding on carcasses, scat varies from black to brown, with mostly hair and some bones. When feeding in alpine areas may contain only parts of moths. Ants often found in scat. Tips have a short taper or are blunt.

blunt end

scat
10 x 1.5 in
25 x 3.8 cm

body rub area

Habitat: High forests to alpine tundra meadows. Stays close to cover, foraging at forest-meadow edge.

Similar species: Differs from black bear by flatter arc of toes, longer claws, and webbing. Differs from wolverine by having toes tightly packed and having a wedge-shaped interdigital pad. Differs from wolf and lion by having five toes.

Other sign: Claws trees, rips open logs, digs into ant piles, digs out roots and rodent caches, and turns over rocks and scat as it look for insects. Rubs body against tree trunks, smoothing bark and leaving hair.

side lope

lope

amble

little toe — web — broad, long claws

big toe

front
5.5 x 5 in
13.8 x 12.5 cm

arch

hind
10 x 6 in
25 x 15 cm

FRONT TRACK LENGTH

HALF FRONT TRACK WIDTH

Black Bear
Ursus americanus

Calf-sized bear, female averaging about 120 lb (54 kg) and male about 300 lb (135 kg). Male grows faster and obtains larger size than female. Color varies from black to brown to blond to red.

Track: Claws on front foot, seldom longer than toes, are usually present. Little toe is set back from rest of toes. Hind print has a large, human-like heel. Outside toe is larger than others.

Trail: Walking stride is 35–40 in (90–100 cm). Usually ambles, a fast walk where the hind foot oversteps the front. Gait is pigeon-toed. Lopes in a C-shaped pattern or a side gallop.

Scat: Normally contains vegetation and is sweet-smelling. When feeding on carcasses, scat varies from black to brown, with mostly hair and some bones. When feeding in alpine areas may contain

scat
7 x 1 in
17.8 x 2.5 cm

hind ___ claws

front claws

claw marks on tree

only parts of moths. Ants often found in scat. Tips have a short taper or are blunt.

Habitat: Forest, seldom venturing far into wide openings. Thick understory vegetation and abundant food sources are critical.

Similar species: Differs from grizzly bear by smaller size, shorter claw length, and more curved arc of toes. Differs from wolverine by having toes tightly packed and having a wedge-shaped interdigital pad. Differs from lion and wolf by having five toes.

Other sign: Claws trees, rips open logs, digs into ant piles, and turns over rocks and scat as it looks for insects, but seldom digs out roots.

side lope

lope

faint little toe

big toe

front
4.5 x 4 in
11.3 x 10 cm

arch

hind
7 x 3.5 in
17.8 x 8.8 cm

amble

FRONT TRACK LENGTH

FRONT TRACK WIDTH

Beaver
Castor canadensis

Largest rodent in North America, 30–60 lb (14–27 kg). Distinguished by large, webbed hind feet and large, horizontally flattened tail. Fur overall is dark brown to almost black, with lighter belly.

Track: Front and hind feet show five toes. Hind foot may be larger than a human hand. Webbing between hind toes shows, but only when pulled tight by splaying of toes. Clear tracks are difficult to find, as the hind foot steps on the front foot and the dragging tail obliterates many prints.

Trail: Walking stride is 18 in (46 cm).

Scat: Seldom found, as they are usually deposited in water, where they disintegrate quickly. Marshmallow-sized, a little longer than thick. Consist of wood chips.

scat
1 x 0.7 in
2.5 x 2 cm

wood chips

Habitat: Seldom found far from a creek, river, pond, or lake.

Similar species: Differs from other rodents by large size and webbing. Differs from river otter by long, slender toes and pointed heel, and by lacking a chevron-shaped pad.

Other sign: Dams and conical lodges, built of twigs and sticks. Standing, cut-off tree trunks end in a tapered cone. Debarked tree limbs in the water.

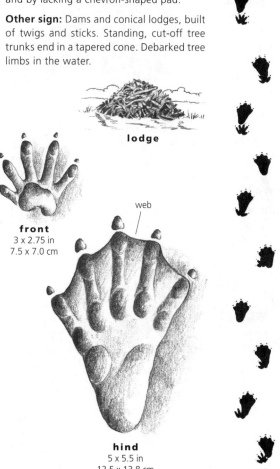

lodge

front
3 x 2.75 in
7.5 x 7.0 cm

web

hind
5 x 5.5 in
12.5 x 13.8 cm

walk

FRONT TRACK LENGTH

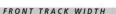

FRONT TRACK WIDTH

Porcupine
Erethizon dorsatum

Basketball-sized
or larger, 10–25 lb
(5–11 kg). Stocky
body, with short
legs. Distinguished
by the presence of
quills. Brown to
yellowish brown in
color.

Track: Rough texture formed by small nubs, on soles of feet. Four toes on front foot and five toes on hind. Toes often do not show.

Trail: Walking stride is 17 in (43 cm). Tail drag often present.

Scat: Winter scat formed from feeding on conifers is red. Summer scat includes

scat
0.5 in
1.3 cm

linked

**debarked
stick with
chew marks**

more herbs and shrubs, and is brown to black. Scat from both seasons may be composed of individual pellets or strings of pellets connected by fibers.

Habitat: Generally found near forests, but may be far from trees if shrubs are available.

Similar species: Rough texture on sole of foot is diagnostic. In snow, trough made by dragging belly highlights its stockiness, separating it from faster-moving mammals.

Other sign: Twigs with bark chewed off, found at the bases of trees. Will perch in a tree for days, chewing the bark, thereby killing the tree.

tail drag

fast walk

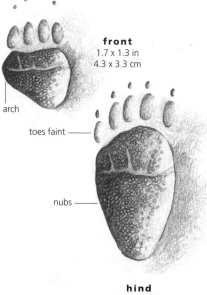

front
1.7 x 1.3 in
4.3 x 3.3 cm

arch

toes faint

nubs

hind
2.7 x 1.7 in
6.8 x 4.3 cm

walk

FRONT TRACK LENGTH

FRONT TRACK WIDTH

Yellow-bellied Marmot
Marmota flaviventris

Size of a large, fat domestic cat, 5–15 lb (2–7 kg). Male larger that female. Ears and head are short and broad. Tail about one-third body length. Color brown to yellowish brown on back, but yellow on belly.

Track: Front foot size of a silver dollar, with four toes in 1-2-1 grouping. Five toes on hind foot, 1-3-1 grouping. Toes relatively slender. Four joined interdigital and two proximal pads on front footprint, and four joined interdigital pads on hind foot. Heel is hairless.

Trail: Bounding stride varies from 24 in (60 cm) to 50 in (125 cm). A ground dweller, the marmot uses a half-bound.

Scat: Wide variety of forms, from oval pellets to long cords, all of which may be tightly stuck together. Sometimes lacks defined shape, being dark and runny when deposited. Deposited in "latrines" or "post offices" on top of prominent rocks and along ledges.

scat
0.25–0.5 in
0.6–1.3 cm

scat on rocks

SCAT WIDTH

Habitat: High mountain areas, especially those with talus and boulder fields. Larger boulders that protect tunnels against digging predators are preferred.

Similar species: Largest of the squirrels, its track dwarfs other ground squirrels. Track left when drinking at a stream may be distinguished from beaver's by lack of webbing and by having only four toes on front prints.

Other sign: May dig tunnels in non-rocky ground between boulder fields, probably as escape tunnels to be used when moving between rocky areas.

— proximal pads

front
2.2 x 1.8 in
5.5 x 4.5 cm

hind
2.8 x 2 in
7 x 5 cm

bound

FRONT TRACK LENGTH

FRONT TRACK WIDTH

Muskrat
Ondatra zibethica

Large, rat-like, stocky, up to 4 lb (2 kg). Males are slightly larger than females. Small eyes and ears. Tail is black, flattened, scaly, with few hairs.

Track: Four toes on front foot (small fifth nubbin may show in very clear tracks) and five on hind foot. Toes very slender. Hind foot appears wider than long.

Trail: Walking strides averages 11 in (28 cm). May lope with body turned to side.

Scat: Oval, at most three to four times longer than wide. Often deposited in a sticky mass on exposed logs at water's edge.

scat
0.2 in
0.5 cm

Habitat: Marshes and lake edges, secondarily on stream banks. Large rivers are not as frequently used.

Similar species: Differs from beaver by smaller size and lack of webbing. Differs from mink by long slender toes and by usually walking.

Other sign: Small conical domes made from reeds serve as dens. Cut grass and reeds near water's edge mark feeding sites. Muskrats make "post offices," repeated scat deposits, on rocks.

4 x 4 bound

3 x 3 bound

side lope

fast walk

walk

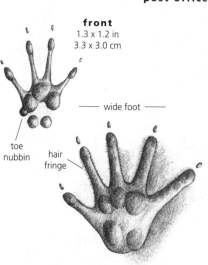

front
1.3 x 1.2 in
3.3 x 3.0 cm

— wide foot —

toe nubbin

hair fringe

hind
1.3 x 1.6 in
3.3 x 4.1 cm

post office

FRONT TRACK LENGTH

FRONT TRACK WIDTH

Prairie Dog
Cynomys species

Blacktail prairie dog
C. ludovicianus

Size of a large guinea pig, 2–3 lb (1–1.4 kg). Fat, yellowish brown ground squirrel. The blacktail prairie dog *(C. ludovicianus)* has a black-tipped tail, the whitetail *(C. gunnisoni)* a white-tipped tail. Lives in large colonies.

Track: Size of a quarter dollar. Long claws on front prints for digging. Four toes on front track, in 1-2-1 grouping (toe 5 does not show). Five toes on hind track, 1-3-1 grouping. Toes are relatively slender.

Trail: Bounding stride averages 30 in (75 cm). Uses a half-bound. Trots more than other squirrels.

Scat: Ranges from oval to a cord five to six times longer than it is wide. Scats are often connected by narrow filaments.

linked

scat
0.1–0.2 in
0.3–0.5 cm

mound and hole

SCAT WIDTH

Habitat: Prairie and open grassland, where colony's "town" may consist of thousands of acres of low dirt mounds concealing tunnels.

Similar species: Differs from ground squirrel by the presence of longer digging claws. Claws longer and broader and feet smaller than those of tree squirrels. Smaller than marmot. Larger than mouse and vole.

Other sign: Colonies consisting of many burrows with elevated mounds and manicured "lawns" of grazed grass.

side lope

bound

long claws

front
1.0 x 0.8 in
2.5 x 2 cm

narrow toes

hind
1 x 0.9 in
2.5 x 2.3 cm

FRONT TRACK LENGTH

FRONT TRACK WIDTH

Pack Rat
Neotoma cinerea

Rat-sized, with a bushy, squirrel-like tail. Averages about 1 lb (0.5 kg). Dusty brown on back, with gray face and whitish belly. Large eyes and ears. Also known as wood rat.

Track: Four toes on front foot, in 1-2-1 grouping. Five toes on hind foot, 1-3-1 grouping. Toes relatively slender. Toe pads are slightly constricted. Three joined interdigital, one remnant, and two proximal pads on front footprint and four joined pads and two proximal pads on hind. Extra pad may show on front print. Feet have considerable hair, sometimes making prints appear indistinct and large.

Trail: Bounding stride is 10 in (25 cm). Walking stride 6 in (15 cm). Bound is probably the most common gait, but walk is also common.

Scat: Small oval pellets.

Habitat: Prefers rocky areas, but will use houses and other human structures when available.

scat
0.2 in
0.5 cm

SCAT WIDTH

Similar species: Larger than mouse and vole. Differs from squirrels by the presence of heel pads on hind foot.

Other sign: Piles of sticks, cactus, bones, porcupine quills, and other debris tightly wedged in cracks in the rocks identify the pack rat home. Yes, this is where to look for missing keys, rings, glasses, and false teeth.

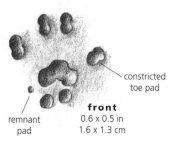

constricted
toe pad

remnant
pad

front
0.6 x 0.5 in
1.6 x 1.3 cm

bound

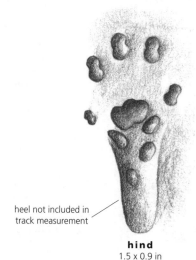

heel not included in
track measurement

hind
1.5 x 0.9 in
3.8 x 2.3 cm

fast walk

FRONT TRACK LENGTH

FRONT TRACK WIDTH

Ground Squirrel
Spermophilus species

Golden-mantled ground squirrel
S. lateralis

Size of a small rat, 0.5 lbs (225 g) and standing 8 in (20 cm) tall. Golden-mantled ground squirrel *(Spermophilus lateralis)* has reddish gold shoulders and neck with white stripe bordered by black on sides of body (no stripes on face). Gray-brown on top of back. Haired tail. Uinta ground squirrel *(Spermophilus armatus)* has light brownish fur spotted with white flecks. Fringe of white hair on edge of haired tail.

Track: Four toes with 1-2-1 spacing on front foot and five with 1-3-1 spacing on hind foot. Toes relatively slender. Front foot size of a quarter. Hind heel is hairless and may register clearly in track. Claws may show.

Trail: Bounding stride averages 15 in (38 cm). Uses a half bound.

Scat: Small ovals, usually not connected.

scat
0.1 in
0.3 cm

burrow entrance

Habitats: Golden-mantled ground squirrel found in mountains with open pine or spruce-fir forest to upper tree line. Uinta ground squirrel found near edges of mountain meadows with open grass. Ranges in elevation to about 8,000 ft (2,400 m).

Similar species: *Spermophilus* species cannot be differentiated from one another by track. Habitat and visual identification necessary. Claws longer and feet smaller than those of tree squirrels. Lack the long claws of prairie dogs. Smaller than marmot.

Other sign: The entrances to golden-mantled ground squirrel burrows are small and found under logs and rocks. Uinta ground squirrels live in colonies which are indicated by many low mounds or moundless burrow entrances.

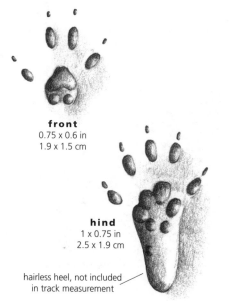

front
0.75 x 0.6 in
1.9 x 1.5 cm

hind
1 x 0.75 in
2.5 x 1.9 cm

hairless heel, not included
in track measurement

bound

Pine Squirrel
Tamiasciurus hudsonicus

Medium-sized squirrel, weighing up to 0.5 lb (225 g). Reddish brown back, separated from white underparts by a black stripe. White ring around eye. Slight ear tufts. Tail is bushy. Also known as red squirrel, tree squirrel, or chickaree.

Track: Front foot size of a quarter, with four toes in 1-2-1 grouping. Five toes on hind foot, 1-3-1 grouping. Toes relatively slender. Claws relatively short. Haired hind heel is indistinct in tracks.

Trail: Bounding stride averages 24 in (60 cm). Tends to use a full bound.

Scat: Small, shapeless black masses to small, usually unconnected ovals.

scat
0.1 in
0.3 cm

chewed cones and seed casings

SCAT WIDTH

Habitat: Boreal or northern coniferous forests. Infrequently found in deciduous forests.

Similar species: Larger than chipmunk. Lacks the long claws of prairie dog and ground squirrel. Smaller than marmot.

Other sign: Builds twig-and-leaf nests in branches of trees, about 15 ft (5 m) from the ground. Piles of pine cone scales (called middens) where squirrel removes scales to get at seeds. Cones are cached deep in the midden for use as winter food.

hind prints
on front

slow bound

claws

pads distinct

front
1 x 1 in
2.5 x 2.5 cm

heel not included in
track measurement

hind
0.9 x 1 in
2.3 x 2.5 cm

full bound

FRONT TRACK LENGTH

FRONT TRACK WIDTH

Northern Flying Squirrel

Glaucomys sabrinus

A small squirrel,
weighing 4 oz (112 g). Its
silky fur is olive-brown
on the back and lead-
gray on the underside. A
fold of skin stretches
between front and hind legs
and body, forming a "wing"
and allowing the squirrel to
glide. Its bushy tail is flattened to aid in sailing.

Track: Front foot size of a quarter, with four toes in 1-2-1 grouping. Five toes on hind foot, 1-3-1 grouping. Toes relatively slender. Claws relatively short and may not show. Hind foot interdigital pads form a tight crescent, though proximal pads are lacking.

Trail: Bounding stride averages 20 in (50 cm). Uses a full bound.

Scat: Small, usually unconnected ovals.

Habitat: Deciduous and coniferous forests, though often found in attics of houses.

scat
0.1 in
0.3 cm

SCAT WIDTH

Similar species: Differs from all other squirrels and chipmunks by the tight crescent of interdigital pads on the hind foot. Lacks the long claws of prairie dogs and ground squirrels. Smaller than marmot.

Other sign: Skin flap outlines may show in dust or snow. Sometimes builds roof on bird nest to use as den. Tree dens may hold 20 individuals during the winter.

hind prints
on front

wing marks

front
0.5 x 0.5 in
1.3 x 1.3 cm

bound

interdigital pads
arrayed in a
crescent shape

hind
1.5 x 0.5 in
3.8 x 1.3 cm

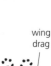

wing
drag

Northern Pocket Gopher
Thomomys talpoides

Hamster-sized,
about 4 oz
(112 g), with
minute eyes and
ears and a short
tail. Has external, fur-lined cheek pouches. Color grayish,
slightly lighter on belly.

Track: Five toes, front and hind feet. Toes relatively slender. Front foot is relatively long, and has long, wide claws for digging. Claw length is equal to or greater than toe length.

Trail: Walking stride is 4 in (10 cm).

Scat: Thick, short cords, about 0.25 in (0.6 cm) long.

Habitat: Meadows from plains to mountaintops.

Similar species: Differs from other rodents by large, strong claws.

Other sign: Summer soil mounds consist of loose dirt forming a flat mound with no entrance visible (gophers close the tunnel

scat
0.2 in
0.5 cm

as they go back underground). When the snow melts, solid casts of soil and rocks show where gophers packed dirt into tunnels in the snow while they burrowed searching for food. Scat is often found embedded in the tunnel casts

dirt cast of winter snow tunnels

prominent claws

fast walk

front
0.6 x 0.5 in
1.5 x 1.3 cm

heel not included in track measurement

hind
0.75 x 0.5 in
1.9 x 1.3 cm

walk

FRONT TRACK LENGTH

FRONT TRACK WIDTH

Ord's Kangaroo Rat
Dipodomys ordii

Stocky and mouse-
sized, about 2 oz
(56 g), with large hind
feet and long fur-
tipped tails. Reddish
brown on back, white
side stripe, and dark
belly.

Track: Hind foot has four toes. Long heel
on hind foot may register. Feet are furred
and toes difficult to distinguish.

Trail: Bounding stride averages 7 in
(18 cm) and typically ranges from 8–16 in
(20–40 cm). Often bounds on hind feet
only. Tail drag often observed.

Scat: Small, usually unconnected, ovals.

Habitat: Low-elevation animal. Prefers sandy soil where it can
easily dig burrows.

scat
0.2 in
0.5 cm

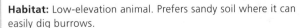

SCAT WIDTH

Similar species: Track differs from western jumping mouse by greater width and more hair. Bounds on the hind feet only; no front prints visible in the bounding pattern.

Other sign: Scrapes out shallow "bathtubs" in dust as it dusts itself for protection against fleas.

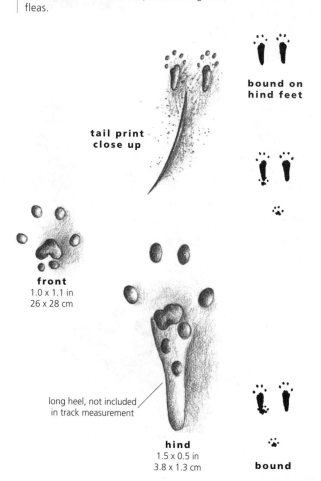

bound on hind feet

tail print close up

front
1.0 x 1.1 in
26 x 28 cm

long heel, not included in track measurement

hind
1.5 x 0.5 in
3.8 x 1.3 cm

bound

Chipmunk
Tamias species

Least chipmunk
T. minimus

Slightly larger than a
large mouse, up to 2 oz
(56 g). Reddish fur, with
white stripes bordered
by black stripes along the
sides of the face and body.
Haired tail.

Track: Front foot size of a nickel, with
four toes in 1-2-1 grouping. Five toes on
hind foot, 1-3-1 grouping. Toes relatively
slender. Claws short. Hind heel is haired
and details are difficult to detect.

Trail: Bounding stride averages 7 in
(18 cm). Mostly terrestrial, it usually uses
a half bound, though full bounds may
be observed in its trails.

Scat: Small, usually unconnected ovals.

Habitat: Varies, including coniferous forest and shrubland. Usually
found near rocks.

scat
0.1 in
0.3 cm

SCAT WIDTH

Similar species: Smaller than ground and tree squirrels. Lacks the long claws of prairie dog and ground squirrel. Smaller than marmot.

Other sign: Seeds and nuts of various plants chewed open on one side.

front
0.5 x 0.4 in
1.3 x 1 cm

furred heel, not included
in track measurement

hind
0.7 x 0.6 in
1.8 x 1.5 cm

half bound

FRONT TRACK LENGTH

FRONT TRACK WIDTH

Voles
Microtus species and *Clethrionomys gapperi*

Many species of mouse-sized mammals, related to lemmings and weighing up to 1 oz (28 g). *Microtus* species are gray to gray-brown

Meadow vole
M. pennsylvanicus

on back, with a light colored belly. *Clethrionomys gapperi,* the red-back vole, has a reddish back. Small, stocky mammals with short ears and small eyes, almost hidden by their fur. Short tails are sparsely haired.

Track: Tracks smaller than a dime. Four toes on front foot, in 1-2-1 grouping. Five toes on hind foot, 1-3-1 grouping. Four joined interdigital and two proximal pads on front footprint and four interdigital pads and one proximal on hind footprint. Heel is hairless.

Trail: Trotting stride is 6 in (15 cm). Usually trot, seldom bound. Tails usually do not show in the trail.

Scat: Oval-shaped pellets similar to those left by house mice, often piled in tennis ball–sized latrines which may hold hundreds of pellets.

scat
0.1 in
0.3 cm

latrine

SCAT WIDTH

Habitat: *Microtus* species are grass-loving species, found near meadows across North America and north to the Arctic. *Clethrionomys gapperi* is found in the evergreen forests of the Rocky Mountains.

Similar species: Differ from shrews by having only four toes on the front feet. Differ from mice by seldom showing a tail drag and by most often trotting. Lack the long heel of the jumping mouse.

Other sign: As snow melts in the spring, grass nests lacking entrances may be found. Snow melt may also reveal 1 in (2.5 cm) cords of grass and debris, stuffed into snow tunnels during the winter to make space elsewhere in the tunnel network. Vole latrines are usually found near nests, while mice leave feces near and in their nests. Worn runways through the grass.

bound

fast trot

trot

front
0.3 x 0.3 in
0.8 x 0.8 cm

hind
0.4 x 0.3 in
1 x 0.8 cm

five pads only

heel not included in track measurement

FRONT TRACK LENGTH

FRONT TRACK WIDTH

Western Jumping Mouse

Zapus princeps

A small—about 1 oz (28 g)—
mouse with long hind feet and
long, sparsely haired tail.
Yellowish sides, darker
yellow-brown back, and
white belly.

Track: Four toes on front foot, in 1-2-1
grouping. Hind foot is about the size of
a quarter, exceptionally long and narrow,
and has five toes in 1-3-1 grouping. Toes
relatively slender. Heel is hairless.

Trail: Bounding stride 60–120 in (150–
300 cm). Makes sharp turns during travel.
May cover considerable distance per stride
when pursued. Tail drag often observed.

scat
0.1 in
0.3 cm

Scat: Small oval pellets.

Habitat: Mountains, seldom found more than 3 ft (1 m) from a stream.

Similar species: Differs from other rodents in having long, narrow hind feet and tail drag. Differs from kangaroo rat by bounding from all four feet, not just hind.

Other sign: Small piles of grass stems left after eating. Round grass nests.

tail drag

front
0.4 x 0.25 in
1 x 0.6 cm

long toes

long heel, not included in track measurement

hind
1 x 0.25 in
2.5 x 0.6 cm

bound

Field Mouse

Peromyscus spp.

Deer mouse
P. maniculatus

Small mouse,
weighing 0.5 oz
(14 g). Adults are
reddish brown on
back with a white
belly, while juveniles are dark gray on the back with a light
gray belly. Large eyes and ears. Tail is long and haired.

Track: Track smaller than a dime. Four
toes on front foot, in 1-2-1 grouping. Five
toes on hind foot, 1-3-1 grouping. Four
joined interdigital and two proximal pads
on front footprint, five joined pads and
heel on hind footprint. Heel is hairless.

Trail: Bounding stride averages 8 in
(20 cm). Those species which use a full
bound are climbers and nest in grass, shrubs, or trees. Those
species using a half-bound nest on or below ground. Both types
occasionally trot. Tail drag may be present.

Scat: Oval-shaped pellets similar to those left by house mice.

scat
0.1 in
0.2 cm

Habitats: Ubiquitous, being found from deserts to the northern tree line, from below sea level to the top of the highest peaks in the Rockies.

Similar species: Differs from shrew by having only four toes on the front feet and by being slightly larger. Differs from vole by showing a tail drag often and by most often bounding. Lacks the long heel of the jumping mouse. Smaller than chipmunk.

Other sign: Compact grass nests without entrances may be found under logs, rocks, and boards. Enters and exits through the grass wall, which closes up after passage. Caches large quantities of seeds in any convenient protected area. Leaves feces near and in nest.

tail
drag

remnant
pad

front
0.3 x 0.3 in
0.8 x 0.8 cm

4 x 4 bound

hind
0.4 x 0.3 in
1 x 0.8 cm

3 x 3 bound

FRONT TRACK LENGTH

FRONT TRACK WIDTH

Shrews
various species

**Smaller than mice,
less than 0.25 oz (7 g).
Long, pointed nose.
Minute eyes and ears. Color
brown to black, with gray to
white belly. Eats mostly insects.**

Masked shrew
Sorex cinereus

Track: Five slender toes are present on front and hind feet. In clear prints, four interdigital and two proximal pads may be seen.

Trail: Hopping stride seldom more than 2 in (5 cm). The group of tracks is less than 1 in (2.5 cm) long. Seldom is the stride more than three times the group.

Scat: Usually small pellets with pointed ends.

Habitat: Found everywhere from deserts to alpine areas. Look for tracks in wet, fine mud of riparian areas or in snow along

——— tapered ends

scat
0.2 x 0.1 in
0.5 x 0.3 cm

insect remains

SCAT WIDTH

logs or the edges of buildings. Wood piles and leaf litter make good homes.

Similar species: Differ from mice and voles by having five toes on front foot.

Other sign: After eating, leave body parts from insects they have killed. Often burrow just below the surface of the snow, opening tunnels that partially collapse and expose their route. Trails in the snow radiate from holes like spokes of a wheel.

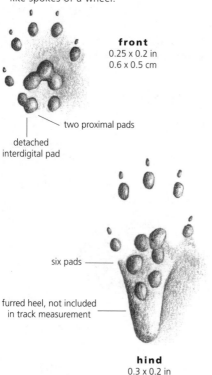

front
0.25 x 0.2 in
0.6 x 0.5 cm

two proximal pads

detached
interdigital pad

six pads

furred heel, not included
in track measurement

hind
0.3 x 0.2 in
0.8 x 0.5 cm

bound

FRONT TRACK LENGTH

FRONT TRACK WIDTH

Bison

Bison bison

Large member of the cow family, with a large shoulder hump and massive skull. Male may weigh 1500 lb (680 kg), female about 1300 lb (590 kg). Head is dark brown to black,

with the rest of the body brown. Calf is red overall. Both sexes have horns that are never shed. Horns of the male are larger.

Track: Very large, with round outer walls. Heavy bulls wear hooves down so much that the division between clouts may not be readily observable. Pad at back of clout forms a v.

Trail: Walking stride is 50 in (125 cm). Usually walks, but occasionally lopes. When stampeding, uses a full gallop, and intergroup distances may reach 10 ft (3 m).

pie

stack

scat
"cow pie" diameter
8 in (20 cm) or greater

female horn

male horn

Scat: Usually moist, forming "cow pies" much of the year. Young bison scat appears as a stack of cookie-sized wafers.

Habitat: Grassland and open mountain meadows. Nowadays, herds are found only in national and state parks, and on private ranches in some areas.

Similar species: Differs from moose track by having rounded wall outline and rounded tips. Larger than other hoofed animals.

Other sign: The most conspicuous sign of the bison is its wallow, a large depression where both sexes roll around, usually in dry dirt, but occasionally in wet areas.

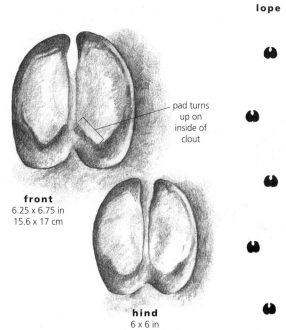

lope

pad turns
up on
inside of
clout

front
6.25 x 6.75 in
15.6 x 17 cm

hind
6 x 6 in
15 x 15 cm

walk

HALF FRONT TRACK LENGTH

HALF FRONT TRACK WIDTH

Moose
Alces alces

Largest member of deer family. Considerable regional variation exists, but male may weigh 900 lb (400 kg), with female smaller. Color varies from tan to blackish. Females have a white patch of hair around the vulva (visible at a distance) that helps identify sex. Male has antlers that are shed annually.

Track: Long, with the pad extending to near the front of the hoof. Subunguinis region is narrow. Track is delicate for the weight of the animal.

Trail: Walking stride is 70 in (175 cm). Seldom gallops. Trots when in a hurry.

Scat: Most of the year, consists of dry pellets that scatter on impact with the ground. When the diet is moist, nipple-dimple shape predominates. Winter scat is oval, and consists mostly of chips of woody vegetation.

scat
0.6 in
1.5 cm

nipple

dimple

SCAT WIDTH

antler

Habitat: Mixed conifer and hardwood forests containing willows and quaking aspen. Streams and shallow lakes provide aquatic vegetation.

Similar species: Differs from elk in that the pad occupies most of each clout. Differs from deer by being larger and more pointed. Differs from bison by having long rather than round track.

Other sign: In removing velvet from their antlers, bulls strip bark from young saplings and break off limbs, often killing the trees. Height of tree wound shows animal height.

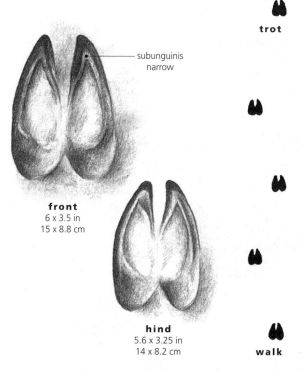

subunguinis narrow

front
6 x 3.5 in
15 x 8.8 cm

hind
5.6 x 3.25 in
14 x 8.2 cm

trot

walk

FRONT TRACK LENGTH

FRONT TRACK WIDTH

Elk

Cervus elaphus

Medium-sized, larger than deer, males averaging 700 lb (320 kg) and females 450 lb (200 kg). Reddish to dark brown, with a yellow rump patch. Males have antlers that are shed annually. Also known as wapiti.

Track: Blocky, with each clout wide at the leading tip. Pad of hoof occupies rear third of each clout; subunguinis occupies remaining two-thirds of each clout.

Trail: Walking stride is 52 in (130 cm). When rushed, gallops and—occasionally—pronks.

Scat: Most of the year, scat consists of pellets that scatter on impact with the ground. When the diet is moist, nipple-dimple shape predominates, changing to oval

nipple

dimple

scat
pellet 0.5 in
pellet 1.3 cm

antler

as drying of vegetation occurs. When scat is moist, pellets stick together.

Habitat: Forest. Beds in dense trees during the day, moving out into clearings to graze during twilight hours.

Similar species: Differs from deer and moose by having a small pad at the rear of the hoof. Differs from bighorn sheep and antelope by having walls that bend to the outside of each clout.

Other sign: In removing velvet from their antlers, bulls strip bark from young saplings and break off limbs, often killing the trees. Height of tree wound shows animal height. Bulls make mud wallows in the fall. During rut, look for areas where bulls have sparred with the ground using their antlers.

pronk

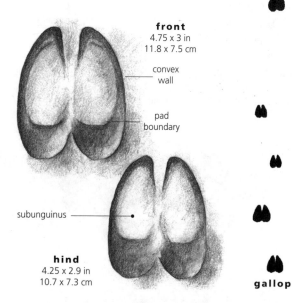

front
4.75 x 3 in
11.8 x 7.5 cm

convex wall

pad boundary

subunguinus

hind
4.25 x 2.9 in
10.7 x 7.3 cm

gallop

FRONT TRACK LENGTH

FRONT TRACK WIDTH

Bighorn Sheep
Ovis canadensis

Medium-sized sheep, distinguished by massive horns of the male. Male averages 300 lb (135 kg), female about 200 lb (90 kg). Light brown, white rump and muzzle. Ram has spiraled horn; ewe's is small and straight. Horns are not forked and are never shed.

Track: Blocky, with edges of the walls straight along the sides.

Trail: Trotting stride is 70 in (175 cm). Most common gait is a walk with 36 in (90 cm) strike, but trotting is common in open country.

Scat: More likely to be dry and to separate into pellets than that of other hoofed mammals.

Habitat: High mountain areas, especially along cliffs. Comes down from cliffs for water, and grazes on grass in rolling hills. Migrates below timberline during the winter.

scat
pellet 0.3 in
pellet 0.8 cm

SCAT WIDTH

Similar species: Wall differs from antelope and deer by having a straight edge. Shows dewclaws, which antelope does not. Differs from deer and elk by relatively large subunguinis region of the clout.

Other sign: Beds scraped in soil along the edges of cliffs; deposits of old scat at repeatedly used beds may be considerable. Mineral and salt licks often serve as a focus of activity.

male horn

female horn

wall straight along sides

front
3.5 x 2.5 in
8.8 x 6.3 cm

hind
3 x 2 in
7.5 x 5 cm

trot

Mountain Goat

Oreamnos americanus

Sheep-sized mammal, found only in North America. Male averages 300 lb (135 kg), female about 200 lb (90 kg). Predominantly white, and distinguished by a stocky build and hump on shoulders. Horns, which are not shed, are straight, about 10 in (25 cm). Those of female slightly smaller.

Track: Footprint is blocky. Tip of the clout occurs in the middle of each clout, not to the inside as in other hoofed mammals. Relatively large subunguinus.

Trail: Walking stride is about 30 in (75 cm). Goats most often walk.

Scat: Tends to be dry and separate when it hits the ground.

scat
pellet 0.4 in
pellet 1.0 cm

horn

Habitat: High mountains, on the steepest crags and cliffs. May bed among rocks, or in snowbanks or vegetated areas. Caves may be used as shelter from sun or wind. Wind-blown slopes are used for feeding in the winter.

Similar species: Differs from all other hoofed mammals by the location of tip in the middle of each clout.

Other sign: Digs dry wallows (shallow depressions) in the summer. Mineral or salt licks attract activity.

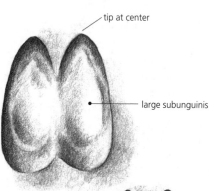

tip at center

large subunguinis

front
3 x 1.9 in
7.5 x 4.8 cm

hind
2.6 x 1.5 in
6.5 x 3.8 cm

walk

FRONT TRACK LENGTH

FRONT TRACK WIDTH

Caribou
Rangifer tarandus

Smaller than elk, larger than deer, with males averaging 250 lb (115 kg) and females about 225 lb (100 kg). The tines (points) over the nose are palmate (webbed). Fur color is gray to grayish brown. Males and females have antlers that are shed annually. Those of males are larger.

Track: Track is wide or wider than long. Hoof walls rounded on the outside, making hoof appear almost circular. Dewclaw impressions are widely spaced.

Trail: Walking stride is 48 in (120 cm). Trotting stride 75 in (188 cm). Caribou walk when grazing, but when moving longer distances, they tend to trot, with hind foot overstepping the front.

scat
pellet 0.4 in
pellet 1 cm

antler

SCAT WIDTH

Scat: Typical scat is dry, falling apart when it hits the ground.

Habitat: The southern limit of range barely reaches the lower 48 states. Habitat includes mountain summits above tree line and alpine meadows interspersed with open sub-alpine forests.

Similar species: Caribou track differs from other hoofed animals by its round, wide print and widely spaced dewclaws. Rounded tips of hoof distinguish caribou prints from those of bison.

Other sign: Large herds leave wide travel route. Snow may be scraped from ground to get at lichens, which caribou eat.

broad hoof

front
4 x 5.2 in
10.9 x 12.5 cm

hind
3.1 x 3.6 in
8 x 9 cm

fast walk

FRONT TRACK LENGTH

HALF FRONT TRACK WIDTH

Mule Deer

Odocoileus hemionus

Small member of the
deer family, male
averaging 160 lb
(70 kg) and female
about 130 lb (60 kg).
Coat color is reddish
brown in summer and
grayish brown in the
winter. Antlers, found
only on males, branch
symmetrically and are
shed annually.

Track: Heart-shaped, with convex wall.
Pad occupies most of the clout;
subunguinis slender.

Trail: Walking stride is 36 in (90 cm).
Pronks or stots with front and hind feet
striking the ground at the same time.
Gallops when in a hurry.

Scat: Usually dry, falls apart when lands
on the ground. Pellets vary from nipple-dimple shape to oval.

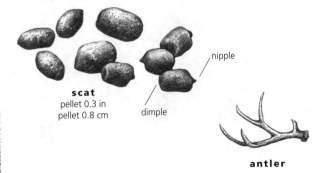

scat
pellet 0.3 in
pellet 0.8 cm

nipple

dimple

antler

SCAT WIDTH

Habitat: Foothills are prime habitat, where can frequent open brush interspersed with rugged terrain. Found in all vegetation zones except in the Arctic and in extreme desert.

Similar species: Track is not distinguishable from white-tailed deer, although mule deer is usually larger. Differs from pronghorn, goats, and sheep by having convex walls. Smaller than elk, has more slender tips, and pad occupies most of clout.

Other sign: Breaks off limbs of trees when removing the velvet from antlers. Velvet is difficult to find, as both deer and rodents eat the nutrient-rich material. Height of tree wound indicates height of animal.

pronk

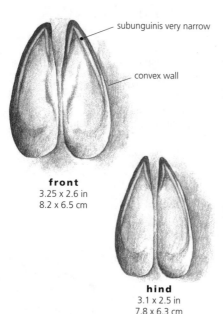

subunguinis very narrow

convex wall

front
3.25 x 2.6 in
8.2 x 6.5 cm

hind
3.1 x 2.5 in
7.8 x 6.3 cm

gallop

FRONT TRACK LENGTH

FRONT TRACK WIDTH

White-tailed Deer
Odocoileus virginianus

Smallest member of the deer family. Male averages 130 lb (60 kg), with female about 110 lb (50 kg). Coat is reddish in summer and blue-gray in winter. The prominent white tail is carried erect when animal disturbed. Antler, found only on male, has tines, or points, branching off main beam.

Track: Heart-shaped, with convex wall. Pad occupies most of the clout; subunguinis slender.

Trail: Walking stride is 30 in (75 cm). Pronks or stots with front and hind feet striking the ground at the same time. Gallops when in a hurry.

Scat: Usually dry, falls apart when strikes the ground. Pellets vary from nipple-dimple shape to oval.

nipple   dimple

scat
pellet 0.3 in
pellet 0.8 cm

antler

SCAT WIDTH

Habitat: Generally closed timber, but moves out to grasslands at twilight to feed.

Similar species: Track is not distinguishable from mule deer, although whitetail is usually smaller. Differs from pronghorn, goats, and sheep by having convex walls. Smaller than elk, has more slender tips, and pad occupies most of clout.

Other sign: Gathers ("yards up") in large numbers in sheltered groves during the winter. Breaks off limbs of trees when removing the velvet from antlers. Velvet is difficult to find, as both deer and rodents eat the nutrient-rich material. Height of tree wound indicates animal height.

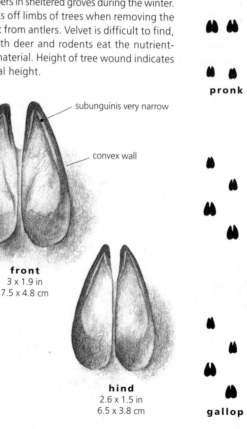

subunguinis very narrow

convex wall

front
3 x 1.9 in
7.5 x 4.8 cm

hind
2.6 x 1.5 in
6.5 x 3.8 cm

pronk

gallop

FRONT TRACK LENGTH

FRONT TRACK WIDTH

Pronghorn Antelope

Antilocapra americana

Smaller than deer;
found only in North
America. Male
averages 125 lb
(56 kg), female about
110 lb (50 kg). White
and tan to reddish
brown, with black and
brown markings on
the head and neck.
Male has forked horns
that are shed annually.

Track: Identified by the concave outline of the wall, which bends slightly inward at a point about one-third of the way back from the tip. Pad is bulbous.

Trail: Ambling stride is 35 in (88 cm). Most common gait is an amble, a fast walk where the hind foot registers slightly in front of the front footprint. Often uses a Z-shaped gallop, with a stride ranging from 80–145 in (200–363 cm).

scat
pellet 0.3 in
pellet 0.8 cm

paw

urine

scat

"spud"

Scat: Typically, well-defined pellets that often stay together upon impact with the ground.

Habitat: Open and shrub country of short- to mid-grass prairie. Herbs and winter browse above the snow are important. Commonly found with sagebrush.

Similar species: Differentiated from deer by its small size and concave wall. Lacks dewclaws.

Other sign: The territorial marking of the male pronghorn is a **spud,** produced as the male **s**niffs and **p**aws the ground after **u**rinating and **d**efecating to spread the odor.

gallop

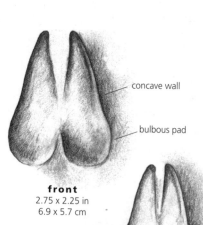

concave wall

bulbous pad

front
2.75 x 2.25 in
6.9 x 5.7 cm

hind
2.25 x 2 in
5.7 x 5 cm

amble

FRONT TRACK LENGTH

FRONT TRACK WIDTH

Trumpeter Swan
Cygnus buccinator

Large aquatic bird, length averaging 60 in (150 cm). Male larger than female. Adult is all white, with a black beak. Immature swan has gray plumage. Male and female identically colored.

Track: Four toes. Toes 2–4, which point forward, usually register. Toe 1 points rearward and only occasionally shows. Distal webbing between toes 2, 3, and 4. Toes 2 and 4 tend to converge slightly near tips. Claws are broad, blunt, and attached to toes. Feet turned in.

Trail: Walking stride is about 14 in (35 cm).

Scat: Cord, five to eight times longer than wide. Often greenish and coated with white nitrogen deposits.

Habitat: Ponds, lakes, slowly flowing streams, and rivers.

scat
3.5 x 0.5
8.8 x 1.3 cm

SCAT WIDTH

Similar species: Larger than ducks and geese. Differs from pelican and cormorant by lacking webbing between toes 1 and 2. Larger than gulls, also differing from them by having convergent toes and distal webbing.

Other sign: Nests on elevated areas such as beaver lodges and muskrat houses, or on the ground. Eggs larger than eggs of Canada goose.

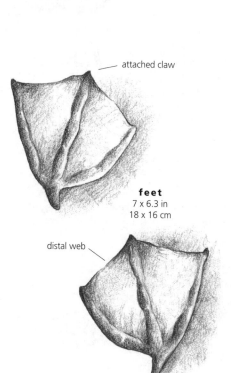

attached claw

feet
7 x 6.3 in
18 x 16 cm

distal web

walk

Great Blue Heron
Ardea herodias

Large wading bird, length averaging 45 in (114 cm). Male and female similar in overall appearance: gray-blue body, with white neck and yellow beak. Black crown extends on feathers off rear of head.

Track: Four toes, toes 2–4 pointing forward. Small proximal web between toes 3 and 4. Footprint is asymmetrical, with toe 1 set to inside of foot axis (drawn through toe 3). Toe 1 is about 1.5 in (4 cm); toe 2 is longer than 1, though shorter than 3 and 4. On hard ground, metatarsal pad may not show (that is, toes may appear unconnected).

Trail: Walking stride about 20 in (50 cm). Trail is fairly straight and feet point forward.

cough pellet

nest

rookery

Scat: Semiliquid, predominantly white. Solid cords of scat vary from 2–3 in (5–7.5 cm) in length, and contain fish, frogs, salamanders, and even small rodents. Ground beneath nests becomes coated with droppings.

Habitat: Frequents backwater eddies along river shores and shallow edges of lakes.

Similar species: Differs from other shore-edge tracks by large size and asymmetrical placement of toes.

Other sign: Large colonies of nests high in trees. Undigested material may be coughed up as pellets.

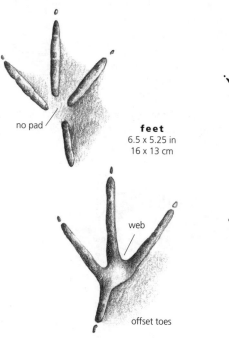

no pad

feet
6.5 x 5.25 in
16 x 13 cm

web

offset toes

walk

HALF TRACK LENGTH

HALF TRACK WIDTH

Sandhill Crane
Grus canadensis

Large bird, length averaging 39 in (100 cm). Appearance of males and females similar: grayish, with red crown on head, and white cheeks and chin.

Track: Four toes, toes 2–4 showing. Outside toes opposed by nearly 180 degrees. Toe 3 is longer than 2 and 4. Small proximal web between toes 2 and 3 rarely shows. Claws usually attached to toes, though claw of toe 1 rarely shows. Feet point forward.

Trail: Walking stride is about 24 in (60 cm). Often runs, extending its stride. Tracks have a narrow straddle, being nearly in line with with one another.

Scat: Similar to, but smaller than, Canada goose. Brown in color, with some vegetation. Can contain bones of small mammals, reptiles, and amphibians.

scat
2.5 x 0.3 in
6.3 x 8 cm

SCAT WIDTH

Habitat: Meadows, marshes, grasslands, and fields.

Similar species: Differs from ducks, geese, swans, and herons by having only small proximal web. Differs from large raptors by lacking toe 1. Larger than most other birds in the Rocky Mountain region.

Other sign: Listen for its rattling call, suggesting to some what dinosaurs may have sounded like.

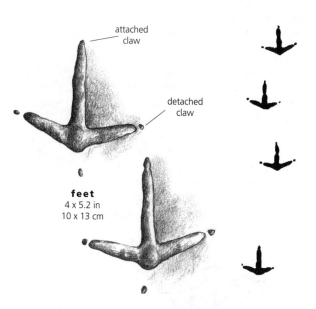

attached claw

detached claw

feet
4 x 5.2 in
10 x 13 cm

walk

Eagles
various species

Large birds, averaging
35 in (90 cm) in length,
with wingspans of 80 in
(200 cm). Brown
bodies. Adult golden
eagle *(Aquila
chrysaetos)* has golden
feathers over head and neck.
Adult bald eagle *(Haliaeetus leucocephalus)*
has white head, neck, and tail feathers.

Bald eagle
Aquila chrysaetos

Track: Four wide, robust toes. Toes 2–4 point forward. Lacks webbing and metatarsal pad. Claws are long, sharp, and not attached to the toe print.

Trail: Walking stride about 18 in (45 cm). Golden eagle will run after prey on the ground.

Scat: Semiliquid, primarily white with some brown intermixed.

Habitat: Golden eagle is found in mountainous areas, and hunts over open country. Bald eagle is usually found near lakes and rivers.

cough pellet

**urine stain
on rock**

Similar species: Larger than hawks. Differ from owls by having three toes pointing forward. Differ from geese and swans by lacking webbing. Differ from herons and cranes by having symmetrical feet.

Other sign: Cough pellets may be 5 x 1.5 in (12.5 x 3.8 cm). Nests may be 6 ft (2 m) in diameter.

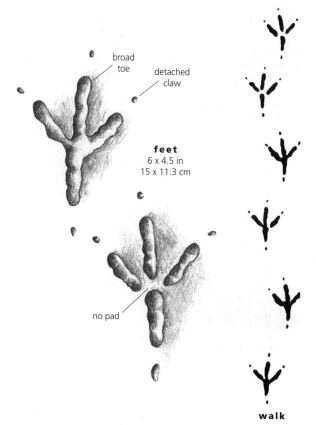

broad toe

detached claw

feet
6 x 4.5 in
15 x 11.3 cm

no pad

walk

Owls
various species

Considerable size variation, from the saw-whet owl *(Aegolius acadicus)*, 8 in (20 cm), to the short-eared owl *(Asio flammeus)*, 15 in (38 cm) to the great gray owl *(Strix nebulosa)*, 25 in (64 cm). All species have immobile eyes offset by facial disks of feathers. Great variability in appearance between species. Typical body colors are grays, browns, and reddish browns.

Short-eared owl
Asio flammeus

Track: Four broad toes, with two paired and facing forward. Toe 4 position is not fixed and may face back or out. Lack webbing and metatarsal pads. Claws long and detached from footprint. Track illustration shows great horned owl *(Bubo virginianus)*.

Trail: Walking stride varies considerably among species, from 3 in (7.5 cm) to 10 in (25 cm).

cough pellet

perch branch

cough pellets

perch with pellets

Scat: Semiliquid, primarily white.

Habitat: Forested areas. Some species, such as barn owls, will readily use human structures.

Similar species: Differ from most birds in toes 2 and 3 being paired, nearly parallel, and pointing forward. Differ from woodpeckers by toes being wide and robust, and by toes 1 and 4 being much shorter than toes 2 and 3.

Other sign: Cough pellets below a roost. Diameter of cough pellets ranges from 0.25–1 in (0.6–2.5 cm) and is directly related to the size of the owl. Pellets are shiny and black when new but turn gray with age.

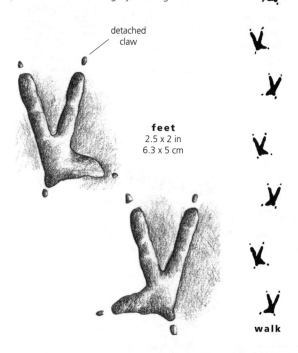

detached claw

feet
2.5 x 2 in
6.3 x 5 cm

walk

TRACK LENGTH

TRACK WIDTH

Canada Goose
Branta canadensis

Medium-sized aquatic
bird, length averaging
30 in (75 cm).
Considerable size
variation among
subspecies. Black head
and neck, with a white
chin band. Back is
olive-brown. Male and
female similarly colored.

Track: Four toes. Toes 2–4, which point forward, usually register. Toe 1 points rearward and only occasionally shows. Distal webbing between toes 2, 3, and 4. Toes 2 and 4 tend to converge slightly near tips. Claws are broad, blunt and usually attached to toes. Feet turned in.

Trail: Walking stride is about 12 in (30 cm).

scat
3 x 0.4 in
7.5 x 1 cm

SCAT WIDTH

Scat: Cord, five to eight times longer than wide. Often greenish and coated with white nitrogen deposits. As long as 3.5 in (8.8 cm).

Habitat: Ponds, lakes, marshes, streams, and rivers.

Similar species: Larger than most ducks and smaller than swans. Differs from pelican and cormorant by lacking webbing between toes 1 and 2. Larger than gulls, also differing from them by having convergent toes and distal webbing.

Other sign: Nests on ground, sometimes on cliff ledges, and in abandoned heron and raptor nests. Eggs larger than chicken eggs.

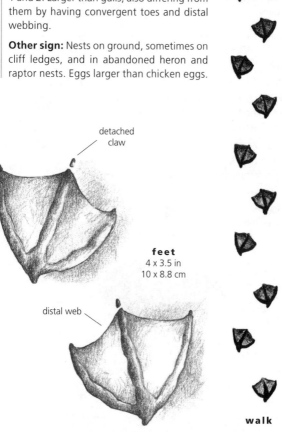

detached claw

feet
4 x 3.5 in
10 x 8.8 cm

distal web

walk

TRACK LENGTH

TRACK WIDTH

Common Raven

Corvus corax

Large black bird, length
averaging 24 in (60 cm).
Beak heavy. Tail is wedge-
shaped in flight. Size
varies considerably,
though male is larger than
female.

Track: Four toes, toes 2–4 facing forward.
Length of toe 1 nearly equals toes 2, 3,
and 4. Lacks webbing and metatarsal pad.
Claws long and detached from footprint.

Trail: Walking stride varies considerably,
but is about 20 in (50 cm). Also runs, with
a longer stride.

Scat: Semiliquid, brown, black, and white.
Often oily. May contain remnants of its
omnivorous diet.

Habitat: Mountains, especially where carcasses of deer and elk
can be found, and at garbage dumps. Will beg food from
picnickers.

cough pellet

Similar species: Track and trail of the common crow are diminutive versions of the raven's. Lacks the paired forward facing toes of owls. Lacks the long toe 1 of hawks. Smaller than eagles.

Other sign: Cough pellets up to 3 x 0.5 in (7.5 x 1.3 cm). Caches food in forks of trees and, often, by burying.

detached claw

feet
3.8 x 2 in
9.5 x 5 cm

no pad

hop

walk

TRACK LENGTH

TRACK WIDTH

Ducks

various species

Mallard
Anas platyrhynchos

Aquatic birds with webbed feet, varying in size from the small bufflehead through mallards to pintails. Length ranges from 14–24 in (35–60 cm). Large variety in body patterns among species. Males generally more brightly colored than females.

Track: Four toes. Toes 2–4, which point forward, usually register. Toe 1 points rearward and may not show. Distal webbing between toes 2, 3, and 4. Webbing concave between toes. Toes 2 and 4 tend to converge near tips. Claws are broad, blunt, and attached to toes. Feet turned in.

Trail: Walking stride of a mallard *(Anas platyrhynchos)* is about 4 in (10 cm).

scat
2 x 0.25 in
5 x 0.8 cm

SCAT WIDTH

Scat: Pencil-sized cords, four to eight times longer than wide. Often greenish and coated with white nitrogen deposits.

Habitat: Ponds, lakes, marshes, streams, and rivers.

Similar species: Tracks differ from geese and swan tracks by smaller size. Differ from pelicans and cormorants by lacking webbing between toes 1 and 2. Differ from gulls by having convergent toes.

Other sign: Nests may be on the ground, in tree cavities, or on floating mats. Eggs roughly the size of chicken eggs, though there may be great variation among species.

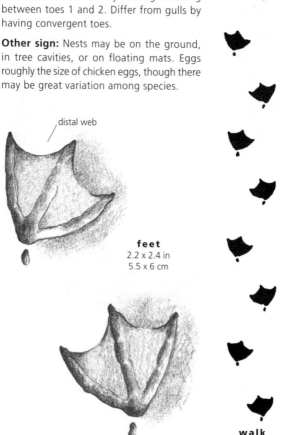

distal web

feet
2.2 x 2.4 in
5.5 x 6 cm

walk

TRACK LENGTH

TRACK WIDTH

Black-billed Magpie

Pica pica

Black and iridescent
green body, wings, and
unusually long tail.
Average length about
20 in (50 cm). Belly is
white. Beak is black.

Track: Four medium-wide toes, three facing forward. Toe 1 nearly as long as toes
2, 3, and 4. Lacks webbing and metatarsal pad. Claws long and detached from
footprint.

Trail: Walking stride is about 6 in (15 cm).

Scat: Semiliquid, brown with white intermixed.

cough pellet

Habitat: Lower mountains, in open woodlands, thickets, along stream edges. Often found near human habitation.

Similar species: Differs from songbirds by larger size and relatively wide toes. Smaller than crows and ravens.

Other sign: Caches food in trees and under bark. Cough pellets are 1.25 x 0.4 in (3.2 x 1 cm).

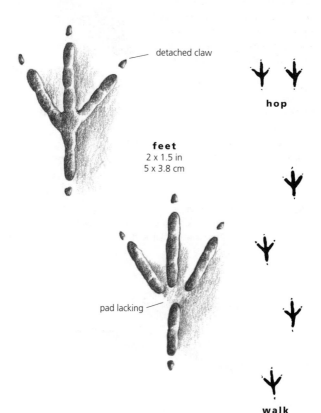

detached claw

feet
2 x 1.5 in
5 x 3.8 cm

pad lacking

hop

walk

TRACK LENGTH

TRACK WIDTH

Grouse

Dendragapus spp.

Blue grouse
D. obscurus

Size comparable to a chicken, 18 in (45 cm) in length. Spruce grouse *(D. canadensis)* is slightly smaller than blue grouse *(D. obscurus)*. Male blue grouse is speckled gray, black, and white, with yellow eye combs. Male spruce grouse is speckled brown, black, and white, with yellow or red eye combs. Males of both species have dark throat. Females are uniformly mottled brown.

Track: Four toes, with toes 2–4 pointing forward. Toe 1, relatively short, may not show. Toes are relatively wide, lack webbing. Feet point forward to slightly inward. In a clear print, a narrow fringe of scales may show around toes.

Trail: Walking stride is about 9.5 in (24 cm).

Scat: Light to dark brown, sometimes with white nitrogenous covering. Content includes buds, berries, and sawdust. In winter, deposited in snow nest in large mass of 50 or so scats.

scat
1.5 x 0.25 in
3.8 x 0.6 cm

SCAT WIDTH

Habitat: Coniferous forest to the upper timberline.

Similar species: Differ from other forest birds by wide, robust toe size and short toe 1. Grouse trails can be differentiated from those of other forest birds by their short strides and wide straddles.

Other sign: Fly into or burrow under the snow to roost. Tunnel to nest makes a sharp turn, perhaps to confuse predators.

broad toe

feet
2.7 x 2.25 in
6.8 x 5.7 cm

walk

TRACK LENGTH

TRACK WIDTH

Shorebirds

various species

Many birds, such as
sandpipers, killdeer,
curlews, and snipes.
Average length varies from
6–18 in (15–45 cm). All
have similar footprints and
differentiation is difficult.

Spotted sandpiper
Actitis macularia

Track: Four narrow toes, although toe 1 may not show. Toes 2–4 face forward and are nearly symmetrical around toe 3. Outer toe angle often greater than 120 degrees. Small, proximal webbing between toes 2, 3, and 4 may be visible, though curlews and sandpipers have proximal webbing only between toes 3 and 4.

Trail: Shorebirds are constantly running along the water's edge. Stride varies from 4–20 in (10–50 cm).

Scat: Small and semiliquid. Browns, green and white mixed.

beach with beak holes

Habitat: Water's edge at lakes, rivers, streams, wastewater treatment plants.

Similar species: Differ from song- or perching birds by the weak showing of toe 1, which in perching birds is strong and used to grasp branches. Outer toe angle of songbirds is less than 90 degrees. Shorebirds walk, but most songbirds hop.

Other sign: Myriad roundish holes where beak pushed into the sand in pursuit of insects.

feet
1.25 x 1 in
3.1 x 2.5 cm

walk

TRACK LENGTH

TRACK WIDTH

Coot
Fulica americana

Medium-sized
aquatic bird, average
length 15 in (38 cm).
Slate-black body, with
white beak extending
into small brown
forehead shield.

Track: Four toes showing, toes 2–4 pointing forward. Toe 1 angles inward. Toes 2, 3, and 4 have fringe of webbing with indented lobes. Long, pointed claws, especially those on toe 1, may be separated from toes.

Trail: Walking stride is 10 in (25 cm). Tends to wander when walking. Foot axis is aligned parallel to line of travel.

Scat: White liquid.

Habitat: Freshwater lakes and ponds having shallow water where reeds and rushes grow.

Similar species: Differs from all other aquatic birds by the indented lobes on each toe.

Other sign: Floating nest built from cattails, sedges, and rushes, rising several inches above the water.

feet
5.2 x 4.8 in
13 x 12 cm

lobe

walk

Northern Flicker
Colaptes auratus

Medium-sized woodpecker, slightly larger than the American robin, with an average length of 12 in (30 cm). Male has brown-barred back, black chest, white rump, red or black whisker stripe, and is red or orange under wings. Female lacks whisker stripe.

Track: Four toes with two parallel and pointing forward. Toes 1 and 4 point backward and are not equal in length. Strong, rigid tail feathers may show on ground.

Trail: Walking stride is about 3 in (7.5 cm). Hopping stride is about 4 in (10 cm).

Scat: Cord, about four times longer than wide. Often contains undigested parts of insects.

Habitat: Open woodlands, cottonwood bottoms, and around towns.

Similar species: Differs from three-toed woodpecker by presence of toe 1. Differs from other birds its size by having two toes pointing forward.

scat
1 x .25 in
2.5 x 0.6 cm

SCAT WIDTH

Other sign: Excavates and nests in tree cavities. Does not add bedding material to cavity nest.

tree with beak holes

toes point
forward

feet
1.75 x 0.75 in
4.4 x 1.9 cm

walk

TRACK LENGTH

TRACK WIDTH

White-tailed Ptarmigan

Lagopus leucurus

At an average
length of 12 in
(30 cm), slightly
larger than the
American robin.
Male and female
similarly colored:
brown- or black- and-white–mottled body in summer, with
white wings. All white in winter. White outer tail feathers in
all seasons. Red eye combs.

Track: Four toes, toes 2–4 pointing forward. Toe 1, relatively short, may not
show. Toes are relatively wide and lack
webbing. In winter the heavily feathered
foot shows broad, diffuse toe imprints,
and detail may be masked. Feet point
forward to slightly inward.

Trail: Walking stride is about 6 in (15 cm).

Scat: Light to dark brown, sometimes with white nitrogenous
covering. Includes buds, berries, and sawdust. About 1.5 in
(3.8 cm) long. In winter, deposited in snow nest in large mass
of 50 or so scats.

scat
1.25 x 0.25 in
3.3 x 0.6 cm

**snow nest and
wing marks
from take-off**

SCAT WIDTH

Habitat: Rocky alpine slopes, meadows, and willow patches of high mountains.

Similar species: Differs from other forest birds by wide, robust toes and short toe 1. Trail shows short strides and wide straddle. Feathers on feet differentiate from other forest birds. Toe angle is narrower than grouse.

Other sign: Flies into or burrows under the snow to roost.

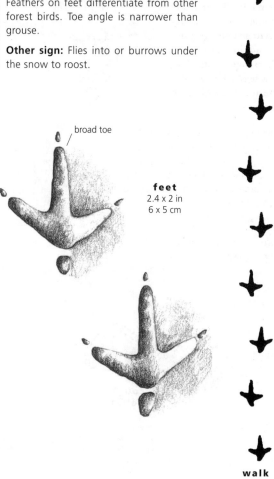

broad toe

feet
2.4 x 2 in
6 x 5 cm

walk

TRACK LENGTH

TRACK WIDTH

California Gull

Larus californicus

Medium-sized bird of the lake edges, average length 8–10 in (20–25 cm). Adult male and female similarly colored: medium gray on back and wings, wing feathers tipped with black. Yellow legs, white chest and head. Yellow bill with red dot.

Track: Four toes. Only toes 2–4 (forward-pointing) show. Distal webbing between toes 2, 3, and 4. Webbing relatively straight between toes. Toes 2 and 3 tend to diverge, especially at tips. Feet turned slightly inward.

Trail: Walking stride is 4 in (10 cm).

Scat: Semiliquid. Primarily white, with indistinguishable contents.

bones and fish scales

cough pellet

Habitat: Mountain lakes, cultivated fields, and landfills.

Similar species: Differs from ducks, swans, and geese by having divergent toes. Smaller than swans and geese. Differs from coot by having webbing between toes. Great variations in stride exist among gull species.

Other sign: Cough pellets are up to 4 in (10 cm) long. Pellets include a variety of materials, reflecting the gull's omnivorous diet.

toes 2 and 4 diverge

feet
1.4 x 1.6 in
3.5 x 4 cm

walk

TRACK LENGTH

TRACK WIDTH

Tiger Salamander

Ambystoma tigrinum

Hot dog–sized salamander, up to 9 in (23 cm) long. Moist, smooth skin. Body brown to black to dark green, with yellow spots or streaks. Tubercles on underside of foot. The only salamander of the high mountains.

Track: Four toes on front foot (often only three show), and five toes on hind foot. The outline of the foot may not show, just toe prints. Even in a clear print, tubercles rarely show.

Trail: Walking stride is about 3 in (7.5 cm). Trail has a wide straddle relative to stride, and may show oscillating belly and tail drag marks.

scat
0.1 in
0.3 cm

egg mass

Scat: Soft, pea-sized black masses with some hint of oval shape.

Habitat: Quiet waters around lakes, ponds, and streams in grassland meadow areas and forests. Found to 9,200 ft. (2,760 m).

Similar species: Differs from lizards by wider, oscillating tail drag and by having only four toes on front foot.

Other sign: Eggs in egg masses are attached individually to underwater plant stems.

front
0.6 x 0.3 in
1.5 x 0.8 cm

hind
0.8 x 0.6 in
2 x 1.5 cm

amble

FRONT TRACK LENGTH

FRONT TRACK WIDTH

Boreal Toad

Bufo boreas

Baseball-sized toad, up to 5 in (7.5 cm) long. Body is light brown to gray to green, with warty skin and dark spots. A white line runs down the back. Female larger than male.

Track: Four toes on front foot and five on hind. Front feet face in. Tubercles on heel of front foot. Four hind toes face in, while one faces out. Two tubercles may show on the heel of the hind foot, and can be confused with toes. Webbing, found only on hind feet, extends at most halfway out to toe tips.

Trail: Walking stride is about 3 in (7.5 cm). Hopping stride generally less than 1 ft (0.3 m).

scat
1 x 0.3 in
2.5 x 0.8 cm

egg mass

toad imprint in mud

Scat: Dark brown to black. Long cord, up to five times longer than wide. Sometimes contains insect parts.

Habitat: Lakes, ponds, beaver ponds.

Similar species: Differs from frogs by presence of tubercles on front heels. Hind foot is narrower than frog. Walks and uses short hops more than the usually long-hopping frog.

Other sign: Long strings of egg masses on bottom and floating among vegetation.

walk

front
0.9 x 0.6 in
2.2 x 1.5 cm

distal web

hind
1.1 x 0.9 in
2.8 x 2.2 cm

hop

FRONT TRACK LENGTH

FRONT TRACK WIDTH

Spotted Frog

Rana pretioas

Baseball-sized frog, 3.8 in (9.5 cm) long. Body light to dark brown, with spots. Spots have light-colored centers. White stripe from jaw to shoulder. Salmon color on lower half of belly.

Track: Four toes on front foot and five on hind. Front feet face in. Four hind toes face in, with one facing out. Webbing, found only on hind feet, is distal, extending most of the way out to toe tips. Toe 1 is thick on male, because it serves as the nuptial pad for grasping female during mating.

Trail: Hopping stride is about 20 in (50 cm). May easily hop 3 ft (1 m) when in a hurry.

Scat: Brown to black, with slightly tapered ends.

Habitat: Cold, nonseasonal ponds, streams, and other water sources. Not found in ponds overgrown with cattails.

scat
1.5 x 0.4 in
3.8 x 1 cm

egg mass

SCAT WIDTH

Similar species: Nuptial pad (enlarged pad for holding female during mating) separates male from other hopping amphibians. Differs from toads by more webbing between toes, lack of palm tubercles on front feet, and by hopping more and at longer distances. Larger than boreal chorus frog.

Other sign: Softball-sized egg masses floating just below water surface.

front
0.8 x 0.5 in
2.0 x 1.3 cm

distal web

hind
1 x 0.8 in
2.5 x 2 cm

walk

hop

FRONT TRACK LENGTH

FRONT TRACK WIDTH

Boreal Chorus Frog

Pseudacris triseriata

Silver dollar-sized frog, less than 1.5 in (3.8 cm). Body brown to green, with three dark stripes on back. Dark stripe through each eye to rump.

Track: Four toes on front foot and five on hind. Front feet face in. Four hind toes face in, with one facing out. Webbing, found only on on hind feet, is proximal, extending at most one-quarter of way to toe tips. Lacks tubercles on front prints. A very clear front print may show enlargement at tips of toes.

Trail: Hopping stride is about 10 in (25 cm). Frogs may easily hop 3 ft (1 m) when in a hurry.

Scat: Firm, black cord with slightly tapered ends.

scat
0.5 x 0.1 in
1.3 x 0.3 cm

egg mass and tadpole

Habitat: Shallow water with emerging vegetation, including pond and lake shores, marshes, and beaver ponds.

Similar species: Lacks the tubercles of the front feet of toad, has less webbing between toes, and hops more and at longer distances. Smaller than spotted frog.

Other sign: Inconspicuous egg masses, consisting of a few eggs in a packet attached to vegetation below waterline.

walk

front
0.6 x 0.4 in
1.5 x 1 cm

proximal web

hind
0.8 x 0.6 in
2 x 1.5 cm

hop

FRONT TRACK LENGTH

FRONT TRACK WIDTH

Snakes
various species

Prairie rattlesnake
Crotalis viridus

A variety of
snakes, from
garter snakes
(*Thamnophis* spp.)
to rubber boas *(Charina bottae)* to bull snakes
(Pituophis catenifer) to prairie rattlesnakes *(Crotalis viridis).*

Track: No footprint to describe.

Trail: Varies from 1–4 in (2.5–10 cm) wide.
Characterized by side-to-side undulations
of the trail. The period, the distance from
one curve to the next, varies by species,
age, and speed of the snake. Surface
material is usually pushed up at the outside of each curve. Gait is either a side-
to-side undulation or sidewinding.

scat
4 x 0.4 in
10 x 1 cm

shed skin

SCAT WIDTH

Scat: Black or brown cord, with constrictions and undulations. White nitrogenous material often attached.

Habitat: Varies widely, from water's edge to rock outcrops to dry sand dunes.

Similar species: Resembles no other track.

Other sign: Shed skin.

**lateral
undulatory**

sidewinding

trail

Sagebrush Lizard

Sceloporus graciosus

Roughly the size of a roll of Life Savers; body less than 2.5 in (6.3 cm), with dry skin and ridged, spiny scales. Gray to brown, with light stripes running length of body. White to light tan belly. Male has bright blue patches on each side of belly and under throat. Female has light blue in same region and salmon color between legs.

Track: Five relatively long, thin toes on front and hind feet. Hind heel is relatively long. Claws may show.

Trail: Running stride is about 3 in (7.5 cm). Hind feet mostly register on top of front feet. Relatively wide straddle. Straight tail drag.

Scat: Brown cord, six to eight times longer than wide. White nitrogenous material usually found on one end.

scat
1.5 x 0.25 in
3.8 x 0.6 cm

Habitat: South facing slopes; warm, open, rocky areas; and forest edges having downed logs.

Similar species: Differs from salamanders by having five narrow toes on front feet and straight trail drag.

Other sign: Scuff marks in dust may indicate a dust bath.

detached claw

front
0.8 x 0.25 in
2 x 0.6 cm

hind
1 x 0.3 in
2.5 x 0.8 cm

amble

FRONT TRACK LENGTH

FRONT TRACK WIDTH

Selected reading

Tracks and tracking

Bang, P. et al. 1972. *Collins Guide to Animal Tracks and Signs*. London: Collins Sons.

Brown, R., J. Ferguson, M. Lawrence, and D. Lees. 1987. *Tracks and Signs of the Birds of Britain and Europe: An Identification Guide*. Kent, England: Christopher Helm.

Brunner, J. 1909. *Tracks and Tracking*. New York: Outing.

Fjelline, D. P. and T. M. Mansfield. 1989. Method to standardize the procedure for measuring mountain lion tracks. In *Proceedings of the Third Mountain Lion Workshop*, ed. R.H. Smith, 49–51. Prescott, Ariz.: Arizona Game and Fish Department.

Forrest, L. R. 1988. *Field Guide to Tracking Animals in Snow*. Harrisburg, Penn.: Stackpole Books.

Halfpenny, J. C. 1997. *Tracking: Mastering the Basics*. 180 min. A Naturalist's World. Videocassette.

——— 1986a. A *Field Guide to Mammal Tracking in North America*. Boulder, Colo.: Johnson.

——— 1986b. *Tracks and Tracking: A "How To" Guide*. Gardiner, Mont.: A Naturalist's World. Slides.

Halfpenny, J. C. et al. 1996. Snow tracking. In *American Marten, Fisher, Lynx, and Wolverines: Survey Methods for Their Detection*, ed. W. Zielinski and T. Kucera, 91–163. General Technical Report PSW-GTR-157. Berkeley, Calif.: USDA Forest Service, Pacific Southwest Research Station.

Headstrom, R. 1971. *Identifying Animals Tracks: Mammals, Birds, and Other Animals of the Eastern United States*. New York: Dover.

Murie, O. 1954. *A Field Guide to Animal Tracks*. Peterson Field Guide Series, no. 9. Boston: Houghton Mifflin.

Rezendes, P. 1992. *Tracking and the Art of Seeing: How to Read Animal Tracks and Signs*. Charlotte, Vt.: Camden House.

Seton, E. T. 1958. *Animal Tracks and Hunter Signs*. New York: Doubleday.

Recommended field identification guides

Burt, W. H. and R. P. Grossenheider. 1964. *A Field Guide to the Mammals*. Peterson Field Guide Series, no. 5. Boston: Houghton Mifflin.

Chandlers, S. R., B. Bruun, H. S. Zim. 1983. *A Guide to Field Identification: Birds of North America*. New York: Golden.

Koch, E. D. and C. R. Peterson. 1995. *Amphibians and Reptiles of Yellowstone and Grand Teton National Parks*. Salt Lake City: University of Utah.

National Geographic Society. 1983. *Field Guide to the Birds of North America*. Washington, D.C.: National Geographic Society.

Stebbins, R. C. 1966. *A Field Guide to Western Reptiles and Amphibians*. Peterson Field Guide Series, no. 16. Boston: Houghton Mifflin.

Index

About the author

JAMES HALFPENNY has searched for dinosaur tracks in Colorado and Montana, tracked wildlife in Tanzania and Kenya, studied endangered species on China's Tibet-Qinghai plateau, and researched the polar bears of Hudson Bay and Greenland. Jim is a member of the International Society of Professional Trackers. Since 1961 he has taught outdoor and environmental education for a vast array of schools and organizations, including the Smithsonian, National Outdoor Leadership School, Outward Bound, the Appalachian Mountain Club, The Wilderness Society, National Wildlife Federation, Defenders of Wildlife, and National Audubon Society. Jim specializes in tracking carnivores, including cougars, wolves, lynx, wolverine, fisher, and marten. He has trained rangers in tracking techniques at Yellowstone, Glacier, Grand Teton, and Rocky Mountain National Parks. His research has also taken him to Antarctica and all over North America. Halfpenny has been featured with Australian aborigines, Kalahari Bushmen, and Alaskan Inuits in a Discovery Channel documentary about the loss of native tracking skills. He is a past field director and project coordinator for the University of Colorado's Institute of Arctic and Alpine Research. He is also the senior author of *Scats and Tracks* series, *A Field Guide to Mammal Tracking in North America, Discovering Yellowstone Wolves: Watcher's Guide, Winter: an Ecological Handbook, Tracking: Mastering the Basics* (video), *Tracking for Elk Hunter's* (video), *Living among Ice Bears* (video), and *A Celebration of Bears* (video). He lives just outside Yellowstone National Park in Gardiner, Montana.

About the illustrator

TODD TELANDER is a freelance natural-science illustrator and wildlife artist. He studied biology and environmental studies at the University of California, Santa Cruz, where he became interested in illustration. His work appears in Falcon's *America's 100 Most Wanted Birds, Birder's Dictionary, A Field Guide to Cows,* and *A Field Guide to Pigs* as well as in museums, galleries, and private collections. Telander lives in Trinidad, California.